A Crown of Candles

How to Throw a Fabulous Lucia Party

JOANNA POWELL COLBERT

"St. Lucia" and "Holly King" artwork by Joanna Powell Colbert.
Ebook design and production by Joanna Powell Colbert, www.gaiansoul.com
Editing by Lunaea Weatherstone, www.lunaea.com
Musical notation by Craig Olson, midwintermoon.bandcamp.com

Photography credits:

Paul Bingman
Pages 6, 8, 11, 25, 26 top, 29 top, 25, 36 bottom, 41, 42, 49 top, 52, 53, 54, 74, 76, 87.

Michele Eva Armstrong, www.hennamoon.com
Pages 26 bottom, 28 top, 31, 32 top, 34, 39, 47, 55 bottom, 57 bottom, 58.

Nora Cedarwind Young, www.thresholdsoflife.org
Pages 16 top, 37 bottom.

Helen Farias
Page 45.

Joanna Powell Colbert, www.gaiansoul.com
Pages 13, 14, 16 bottom, 17, 23, 24, 28 bottom, 29 bottom, 30, 32 bottom, 33 bottom, 36 top, 37 top, 38, 42, 46, 48, 50, 55 top, 56 top, 57 top, 62, 64, 70, 71, 75, 78, 80.

iStockPhoto.com
Pages 24, 44, 77, 79, 81.

Dedicated to

Helen Farias,

who started it all,

And to my co-hostesses and co-hosts in the

Circle of Stella Maris

who co-create our Lucia Parties:
Deep thanks and appreciation.

It takes a community to throw this party!

table of Contents

Lo! on our threshold there,
White-clad, with flame-crown'd hair:
Santa Lucia, Santa Lucia!

I hear you singing this refrain as I enter your homes on this dark night, bearing my gifts of light for your souls and bread for your bodies. Oh, hail! Do you know me? Even my name speaks of the Light. I am Lucia, that one whose visit heralds the return of the sun.

In elder times, you called me by other names. In ancient Rome, I was Juno Lucina, midwife to the newborn sun. In the northlands, I was Freya, she of the golden necklace, bride of the Vanir. I flew across the night sky in an amber chariot drawn by my beloved cats and entered your homes before dawn. My cats came along, though mysteriously changed into nourishing cakes! You knew me too as Frigga of the hearth and home, when I sat at my spinning wheel and spun threads of sunlight to brighten the morning sky.

They say of me: "Honor St. Lucy with great good cheer, and you shall have plenty for all of the year!" And it's true! You do me honor when you gather in my name. I bring to you the gift of the gathering of friends and family, and the promise of longer days.

More than anything, I am the Lightbringer, who appears mysteriously out of the darkest night with hope and sustenance for all.

Preface

Many years ago, I was invited to the legendary Lucia Parties hosted each December by Helen Farias, creatrix and editor of the original *Beltane Papers*. I had never attended anything like it, where a Yuletide party with all its revelry was in full swing, then suddenly interrupted by the arrival of a magical figure with a story to tell and gifts to distribute. She or he then vanished into the dark night. These mysterious appearances brought everyone there closer to a sense of the numinous, an experience sorely lacking in most modern Yuletide festivities. Helen died in 1994, but her parties go on, hosted by friends in Boise, Bellingham, and Seattle.

My spiritual community has continued the tradition every year since 1997 by throwing a large party in St. Lucia's name (she is also called St. Lucy, Santa Lucia, and the Lucy Bride, among other names). We love Lucia because she is a strong, beautiful female icon of the Yuletide season. The sight of her unexpected appearance in the midst of a bustling party, head crowned with blazing candles in the darkened room, never fails to thrill the assembled guests.

I started our parties based on the traditions I remembered from Helen's parties, like the Sweet Room (a room dedicated to cookies and candies) and wassailing the trees. Of course, our community added its own touches. We always have a lot of live music, since we have so many musicians among us, and we often end the evening with a drum circle. Many of the young women who have played the role of the Lucy Bride over the years grew up coming to the parties. My young friend Chloe Eloise, who was the Lucy Bride in 2009, has been to our Lucia Parties almost every year of her life.

My circle of hostesses and I start planning the Lucia Party every year in early October. In this book, I've included everything I can think of to ensure a successful Lucia Party of your own. There are checklists, timelines, menus, recipes, suggestions for party activities, an invitation you can download, song lyrics, and instructions on how to make a Lucia crown. I've also included scripts for the various Numinous Beings that might appear throughout the party.

Of course, you won't create a party exactly like ours. Feel free to use only the suggestions that work for you and your community. And I'd love to hear all about your own special touches.

May Lucia bring light to your hearts and homes,

Joanna

Planning the Party

We usually start planning the party around October 1st. There is a core group of three to five hostesses who do most of the planning, but we ask for a lot of volunteer help. This section outlines the basic information you'll need for planning, including timelines. The details are all in the sections that follow.

Choose the Date

St. Lucia's Day is December 13th, so we try to have the party on the Saturday closest to that day. In practice, it is often the second Saturday in December. This works out quite well, since the third Saturday is usually scheduled for Christmas parties or Winter Solstice celebrations. If you always hold it on the second Saturday in December, your guests can mark their calendars a year in advance. (Believe me, they will!)

The hostesses and I actually mark off the whole weekend on our calendars. We start on Thursday, pulling out boxes, washing and ironing tablecloths, and shining the silver punchbowl. We usually do the grocery shopping on Thursday too. Friday is for decorating the house, and Sunday is for a more intimate gathering of the hostesses and families. We have Sunday brunch together and nibble on leftovers all day. Sometimes those of us who have spent the night don't even get out of our jammies.

Location

My husband Craig and I have hosted the Lucia Party in our home every year since 1997 with two exceptions. In 1999, our friend Nora hosted it in her home, and in 2008, we rented a Victorian house in downtown Bellingham.

The Victorian house was large and beautiful, and parking was not a problem, but it had two main drawbacks. Since it was not someone's home, it felt like a stage set — a lovely one to be sure, but lacking in the personal touches that mark someone's home. A more serious problem was the curfew of 11 p.m., which meant that the party had to end by 10 p.m. in order for us to have time to clean up.

When Craig and I lived on Lummi Island, our house was quite large and we used every single room in it for the party. This meant the guest list could be sizable, and over the years it grew and grew. I think the most guests I ever counted was around 85. Do I need to say it? This is really too many guests for a private house party.

We are now hosting the party at our home in Bellingham, which is much smaller than our island house. We make it work by taking out some of the living room furniture for the party and rearranging the rest. We also rent outdoor heaters so that the deck and backyard can be used. But we still have to seriously limit the guest list.

Guest List

This can be a hard one. Everyone wants to share such a fun occasion, and each of the co-hostesses may want to invite some of her friends. This is a great way to meet new and interesting people, and it helps the community to grow. But we've learned from experience that too many people crowded into too small of a space is not fun for anyone. So you and your co-hostesses will have to make some decisions. When you are counting heads, remember that when you invite single people they will expect to be able to bring a date or a friend. Families grow, adding to the guest list as well. Some of our children now have spouses and children of their own. It's a multi-generational party! Our last guest list was limited to around 45 people, which is how many people can comfortably fit in our house. It's a good idea to invite a few more guests than your maximum number, as it's likely not all of them will be able to attend.

Tasks and Roles

Here's a list of tasks that need to be done and roles that need to be fulfilled. The hostesses take on some of these and ask volunteers to do the rest.

Tasks:

- Review the guest list. Is there anyone who has not attended the last few years? Are there new couples or new children in the community?

- Create and send out the invitations.

- Organize the dinner menu and potluck contributions.

- Decide on the layout of the house and plan to rearrange furniture as necessary. Plan for the dinner table, drinks bar, Sweet Room, stage area for musicians, the route for the Lucy Bride and her train, dressing rooms for the Lucy Bride and other Numinous Beings, and the Snapdragon table (more about these later). You may also want to designate a quiet room for conversation, a kids' area, an outside smoking area, etc.

- Rent outside heaters if necessary.

- Decide on how many Numinous Beings will appear, and who will play them; create and send out scripts to the players.

- Choose other games and activities for the party.

- Arrange for accommodations for overnight guests.

- Organize the menu and potluck contributions for Sunday brunch.

- Housecleaning both before and after the party (I highly recommend hiring someone).

- Gather fresh greenery for decorations and for the Lucy Bride's crown.

- Garden/yard cleanup.

Roles:

- Decorators for the outside of the house.

- Decorators for the inside of the house, including the tree.

- Party flow director: Writes out a loose timeline of the activities.

- Kitchen cleanup facilitator during the party: Encourages guests to help with the cleanup. "Many hands make light work!"

- Fire-tender (if you have an outdoor fire pit, or even a fire in your fireplace).

- Someone to be responsible for background music during the party (i.e., create a Yuletide playlist for the iPod player or keep the CD player stocked).

- Someone to light the Candle of Little Yule and read *The Shortest Day* poem aloud.

- Someone to make the Yule log and lead the men in bringing it into the house.

- Musicians for the mini-concert(s). This is an excellent chance for the kids to share what instruments they are learning, in additional to a concert by the adult musicians in the community.

- Caroling sing-along leader.

- Someone to play the Lucy Bride.

- People to play the various Numinous Beings.

Props

We have collected these things over the years and usually keep them in storage until it's Lucia Party time.

- Plates: We buy them at garage sales or secondhand shops. They are a motley crew, all mismatched, but it's better than buying paper or plastic plates.

- Flatware: Also mismatched and better than plastic.

- Cloth napkins (can be supplemented with paper if necessary).

- Serving spoons (people often forget to bring these). You'll need more serving spoons than you can imagine. Buy them at a secondhand store.

- Wineglasses.

- Other glasses, including unbreakable ones for kids.

- Punchbowls and cups. We usually fill a large punchbowl with ice and place several bottles of wine inside. We use other punchbowls for eggnog.

- Coolers for beer and other drinks, as an adjunct to refrigerators.

- Tablecloths for the dinner table, beverage bar, and surfaces in the Sweet Room.

- Yuletide-themed artwork. We take down some of the framed pieces of artwork that normally hang on our walls and replace them with Yule art.

- Chime or bell to signal activities and the entrance of Numinous Beings.

- Props for the Lucy Bride and train: Lucy's costume, including her crown with fresh greens and real candles; capes or cloaks for the girls in her train; tray for the *lussekatter*; candles in holders for the girls in the train.

- Yule songbooks, 40–50 copies, depending on how many guests you will have.

- Large basket for the gifts for the children.

- Children's games and crafts (paper, glue, etc.), if you have a designated area.

- Lots of votive candles or tealights in jars or holders, for decorations and for an altar.

- Fresh cranberries and popped popcorn for stringing plus thread and needles.

- Cards that say "Vegan," "Vegetarian" and "Gluten-Free" for the potluck table.

- Cards that say "Without Alcohol" and "With Alcohol" for the beverage bar, especially if you're serving two kinds of eggnog (always a good idea).

- Snapdragon game materials: Raisins, brandy, a shallow flameproof bowl, a small table (such as a card table) covered with aluminum foil.

timeline

It's good to get as much done ahead of time as possible, so you and your co-hostesses can enjoy the party as much as the guests do.

One month before the party:

- Create and send out the invitations.

- Make sure all helpers and participants know what they're supposed to do.

- Go shopping for a gorgeous dress or outfit (even if it's shopping in your own closet). This is a "dress your festive best" occasion.

- Make or find a really special gift for the gift exchange (spend no more than $5). Hosts should provide several extra gifts, as there are always people who forget to bring one.

the week of the party:

- Clean house super-thoroughly (hire help).

- Garden/yard cleanup (hire help as necessary).

- Get Yule decorations out of storage.

- Set up outdoor decorations (house twinkle lights, wreath for front door, tiki torches, rope lights, or luminarias for paths).

- Rent outdoor heaters.

- Go get the Yule tree.

- Decorate the Yule log.

- Verify food list and confirm who is bringing what.

- Confirm that the Lucy Bride and her mother have the *lussekatter* recipe.

- Make sure you have all the tableware: plates, flatware, napkins, wineglasses, etc., and that all are clean.

- Make sure you know what you're wearing to the party, and that it's clean and ready to go.

- Grocery shop for the party.

- Buy ice for the coolers and punchbowls that hold bottles of wine.

- Make your potluck items and sweets ahead of time.

- Have guest rooms ready for overnight guests.

- Make sure the bathrooms are stocked with extra rolls of toilet paper.

the day before the party:

- Gather fresh greens to use for decorations.

- Welcome your first overnight guests.

- Clear out some furniture from the main party room and rearrange the rest.

- Set out greenery and votive candles throughout the house, including the bathrooms.

- Decorate the house and Yule tree.

- The Lucy Bride (and her mother, most likely) make the *lussekatter*.

- Be as stress-free as possible, since you've already done most of the work.

the day of the party:

- Set up the Sweet Room with tablecloths and decorations.

- Set up the dinner table with tablecloths, napkins, flatware, plates, etc.

- Set up the drinks bar; put bottles of wine in one large punch bowl filled with ice. Set out all the wineglasses. Set up two more punchbowls plus cups for the two kinds of eggnog.

- Light the candles in the windows just before people arrive.

- Put the background music on.

- Set out appetizers (crackers, nuts, etc.) and the first round of beverages.

- Get dressed and make yourself look beautiful!

- Relax, enjoy, celebrate!

The Invitations

The party begins with the invitation. Every year I swear I'm going to take the time to mail out "real paper" invitations, like we did in pre-email days. But most years I run out of time and fall back on email. However, I do not recommend this.

The invitations set the mood of the party. We want people to dress up and to expect something really, really special — this isn't any ordinary holiday party, you know!

The artwork on the invitation varies from year to year, but the text for it stays pretty much the same. In fact, most of the text for the invitation was written by Helen Farias back in the 1980s for her own Lucia Parties.

Honor St. Lucia with great good cheer and you shall have plenty for all of the year

Here's the text we use. You are welcome to use it for your own invitations.

The Circle of Stella Maris

invites you to our annual

Lucia Party

in honor of the Lightbringer whose visit heralds the imminent return of the sun!

Saturday, December 13th, 20xx
from 3:00 p.m. to midnight (and beyond)

at the home of Craig Olson and Joanna Colbert,
123 Main Street, Bellingham, Washington

*Expect many interesting Occurrences, Activities, and Epiphanies all evening long,
including the Appearances of Numinous Beings!*

Attire: Dashing.

Please bring: A main or side dish, sweets for the Sweet Room, and liquid
refreshment (alcoholic or not). Also bring: A small, wrapped, exquisite gift
(spend no more than $5) for the gift exchange.
(Children's gifts should be labeled with their names.)

Please RSVP to Joanna: (333) 555-9999 / joanna@gaiansoul.com

Space is limited so RSVPs are a must!

Please let Elaine know what dish you'd like to bring for dinner:
(333) 555-4444 / elaine@elainesemail.com

Dinner will be served at 5:30 p.m.

REMEMBER:

"Honor St. Lucy with great good cheer, and you shall have plenty for all of the year!"

Notice that we ask for an RSVP. You would not believe how many people ignore this! But it's essential for knowing how many folks to expect. Also, the time we set for dinner on the invitation is usually 30–60 minutes before we really plan to begin.

Here are samples of two invitations I designed.

(rotated text within image — invitation card)

Honor St. Lucia with great good cheer and you shall have plenty for all of the year

Santa Lucia

Before dawn on December 13, "Little Yule," the eldest daughter
of a Scandinavian household arises and sets a wreath of greenery
upon her head to which are anchored several candles. With these
all ablaze in the pre-dawn dimness she walks the corridors,
calling on each bedroom with a gift of hot coffee, *lussekatter*
("Lucy kats," yeast rolls) and gingerbread. She is the
Lussibruden, the Lucia Bride, Saint Lucy.

Lucia exhbits traits of many ancient goddesses. She is almost
certainly a face of Freya, "Mistress of Cats," whose special season
was Yule and who was dedicated to the dispensing of wealth
and plenty. The Norse sun-goddess Sunna, whose emblem is
the firey wheel, is also present in St. Lucy, and the Italian
midwife goddess of "first light," Lucina, may have lent
her name to this bright figure.

More than anything, Lucia is the Lightbringer,
the Child of Light who appears mysteriously
out of the darkest night with hope and sustenance for all.

Santa Lucia ©2000 Joanna Powell Colbert
www.GaianSoul.com

The Party

As guests arrive, they take their sweets to the Sweet Room, their main or side dish to the kitchen or dining table, and their beverage to the beverage bar. They also give the package they brought for the gift exchange to one of the hostesses. It's important to keep the children's gifts (each marked with their name) in a separate basket so they are easy for the Giftbringer to find later on in the evening.

There should be appetizers and beverages set out for the guests, and they should be guided toward them if they don't do it automatically. (Yes, I know, that's Being a Good Hostess 101.)

Activities

We don't do all of the following activities each year, except for the ones with the asterisks next to them. Those we do every year without fail. It's tradition!

- Wassailing the trees
- Stringing cranberries and popcorn
- Making paper crafts, such as ornaments
- Bringing in the Yule log
- Lighting candles at an altar
- Lighting the Candle of Little Yule, reading *The Shortest Day* poem*
- Toasting the year's passages*
- Appearance of Numinous Beings*

- Arrival of the Lucy Bride*
- Gift exchange*
- The Sweet Room*
- Short tarot or other oracle readings
- Sing-along caroling with songbooks*
- Concert*
- Snapdragon
- Plum pudding
- Storytelling
- Drum circle

See the next chapter for details.

timeline

A loose timeline for the party might look something like this:

BEFORE DINNER: 3–5:30 p.m.

- String popcorn and cranberries; paper-craft ornament making.
- Wassail the trees before dark, 3:30–4 p.m.
- Light the candle of Little Yule and read *The Shortest Day* poem, 5 p.m.
- Men bring in the Yule log OR an appearance of a Numinous Being, 5:15 p.m.

DINNER: 5:30–7 p.m.

- Craig and Joanna welcome the guests and introduce the co-hostesses.
- Sing a blessing song.
- Eat dinner; elders go through the potluck line first.
- After dinner, Joanna leads a toast of the year's passages: births, weddings, deaths, other momentous occasions of the past year.

- A Numinous Being appears.

- Plum pudding and eggnog are brought out.

AFTER DINNER: 7–11 p.m.

- Child or teen musician plays for the company (cello, clarinet, etc.).

- Lucia appears, 7:15–7:30 p.m.

- Giftbringer appears and passes out the gifts, 7:45

- Concert by Craig and Julianne, 8:15

- Sing-along caroling with songbooks, 9:00 p.m.

- A Numinous Being appears, 9:45 p.m.

- Snapdragon, 10 p.m.

- Drum circle, 10:30 p.m.

LATE NIGHT: 11 p.m. until the wee hours

- Drumming, dancing, singing, storytelling

The times on the timeline are just a guideline. The trick to all these activities is to make sure there is plenty of time in between them for people to have conversations and just enjoy each other. If the energy in the room starts to lag, then it's definitely time for the next activity.

We found that it's important to have the Giftbringer come out fairly early, as little children have a hard time waiting and sometimes they fall asleep. Some years we have had several Numinous Beings, and other years we have cut it back to just Lucia and the Giftbringer. We've also found that many guests leave by 11 p.m., so the "late night" activities are often with a much smaller group of people. It's a nice segue into Sunday morning with the small group of hostesses and their families.

Activities in Detail

Wassailing the Trees

Every year at Helen's Lucia Parties, we would all take a cup of wine or apple cider outside before dusk, and gather in her apple orchard to wassail the trees. My memory is a little fuzzy, but I'm pretty sure we sang one of the traditional "Wassail" songs, either "Wassail, wassail all over the town, our toast it is white and our ale it is brown . . ." or "Here we come a-wassailing among the trees so green . . ." We toasted the trees with a sip and then poured the rest out in libations at the base of each tree.

Wassailing comes to us from the British Isles, like so many of our Yuletide customs. The word wassail actually means "Be thou well [or hale]" or "May you be in good health!" Waverly Fitzgerald writes:

"Wassail was originally a drink of spiced ale, with bits of toast (hence our term 'toasting') or whole apples floating on top. The apple was the last harvest of the year and wassail is the drink of this season, from Halloween through Yule, perhaps because the apple is associated with the Celtic Underworld and this is the time of death in the natural world.

"Wassailing refers to both the custom of going around singing carols and expecting to be invited in for strong drink and food, and the custom of pouring a libation to the apple trees, to thank them for the past harvest and ensure a good harvest in the year to come."*

*Waverly Fitzgerald, *Celebrating Yule*, 2003, www.livinginseason.com

When we lived at Heron House on the island, we didn't have any apple trees, or indeed any fruit trees at all. But we did have a Magical Hawthorn Tree. So every year I would tell its story before we sang and poured libations on its roots.

The year that we rented the Victorian house in town for our party, we honored a wonderful old yew tree on the property. (Yew trees are symbols of death and rebirth, so appropriate for the Yuletide season.) Here at Rainbow Cottage outside of Bellingham, we have many western red cedars. There is one in particular that I call Grandmother Cedar, and she is the main tree we honor here. So if you have no apple trees to wassail, choose a tree that is special to you and honor it instead.

Stringing Cranberries and Popcorn

It's nice to have bowls of popcorn and cranberries set out for those guests who arrive in the afternoon and would like a little something to do as everyone arrives and dinner is being prepared. Put a little basket with needles, thread, and scissors next the bowls of popcorn and cranberries. People know what to do! (Be sure the scissors and needles are out of the reach of little children.) Afterwards, they can put the strings on your Yule tree, or the trees outside, or take them home to put on their own Yule trees.

Making Paper-Craft Ornaments

This is another low-key activity that folks can do while waiting for the party to really get into gear. It's fun for the children, too. If you want to keep going with a Scandinavian theme, it's fun and easy to make little heart-shaped woven paper baskets. Just put out the materials (paper, scissors, glue) and a few instruction sheets. It's easy to find instructions on how to make these in craft books or on the web.

Bringing in the Yule Log

If you have a big fireplace, it's great to have a Yule log decorated ahead of time. Cut a log to fit your fireplace, preferably from your wood pile or a tree or limb that is a blow-down. No damaging of live trees allowed! Decorate the log with cedar, holly, ivy, fir, and herbs to make it truly gorgeous.

Have your fire-tender start a fire in the fireplace. Then ask all the men to go outside. The main "Yule log guy" (usually the one who decorated the log) will get them started singing "Deck the Halls" as they carry the Yule log on their shoulders into the house. This is great fun. All the women love cheering them on. It's great to time the placement of the Yule log onto the fire with the verse that starts "See the blazing Yule before us! Fa la la la la la la la la . . ."

Lighting the Candle of Little Yule

This is another one of Helen's traditions. Just around dusk, we ask people to gather round while we light a special candle. I usually buy a new one each year for this (beeswax is my preference). One of us will usually explain that St. Lucia's Day used to be called "Little Yule" in Sweden, and it is the day the Midwinter festival begins. Someone has been chosen ahead of time to light the candle and read the poem *The Shortest Day.* This is often one of the children or a teenager. The poem doesn't have to be memorized, but she or he should practice ahead of time, as it needs a good, dramatic reading. A little coaching never hurts.

The appointed one lights the candle and reads the poem to the guests, and they repeat the last line three times in a call-and-response fashion: "Welcome Yule!" This really kicks off the party!

The Shortest Day
by Susan Cooper, written for the Christmas Revels

And so the Shortest Day came and the year died,

And everywhere down the centuries of the snow-white world

Came people singing, dancing,

To drive the dark away.

. . .

[Use a search engine to find the text of the entire poem. I don't have permission to reprint it here.]

They carol, feast, give thanks,

And dearly love their friends,

And hope for peace.

And so do we, here, now,

This year and every year.

Welcome Yule!

Lighting Candles at an Altar

One year I had an outdoor shrine set up, with votive candles and matches set out. There was also a large ceramic bowl of water with floating candles in it. A sign invited people to "say a prayer and light a candle." It was a lovely little oasis of peace and quiet in the midst of the revelry.

Dinner Blessing

When dinner is ready to be served, with all the dishes laid out on the dining table, the guests gather in one giant circle. It's often an amoeba-shaped circle, but it's important that everyone joins hands to bless the food. Craig and I usually welcome all the guests, very briefly, and thank them for once again blessing our home at the turning of the Wheel. We introduce the co-hostesses and thank them for their hard work. We remind everyone (especially the children) that our elders get in line first to fill their plates.

Then everyone sings this chant, three times:

Harvest Blessing Chant
by T. Thorn Coyle and Starhawk

Our hands will work for peace
and justice,

Our hands will work to heal
the land.

Gather round the harvest table,

Let us feast and bless the land!

toasting the Year's Passages

As dinner is winding down, I ask people to toast the passages of the year gone by — the births, deaths, and weddings of people in our community. It's a lovely way to honor the newlyweds and new babies in the room, and to remember those no longer with us. We always raise a toast to Helen at this time too.

the Sweet Room

In her description of Helen's Lucia Parties, Waverly Fitzgerald wrote this:

"The guest bedroom converted for the night of the party was the Sweet Room, a wonderland of white and glitter, with candles burning amongst boughs of evergreens and plates of cookies, the name of each on a card written in gold calligraphy: *Kourbiedes, Zimsterne, Springerle.*" *

*Waverly Fitzgerald, *Celebrating Yule*, 2003, www.livinginseason.com

Since I need my guest bedroom for overnight guests, I use my studio/office for the Sweet Room. I clear off my art table and other surfaces, and put my desktop computer and printers away. I cover all the surfaces with tablecloths. One year I bought a lot of cotton Christmas-themed yardage, and I use that year after year too.

We decorate the Sweet Room just like we do the rest of the house, with lots of fresh cut evergreens, candles, and other goodies. I like to set out my collection of children's Christmas stories so people can pick them up to read if they like. As the guests arrive, the tables fill up with all kinds of delectable candies, cookies, pies, and cakes. We are likely to label things "vegan" or "gluten-free" instead of the exotic cookie names Waverly remembers. The gold calligraphy is still a lovely idea, though.

There are several chairs in the Sweet Room, and the intention is for it to be a quiet room, where people can have low conversations as they indulge their sweet tooth. It doesn't always work out that way. There have been times when children have gone off on a sugar high and taken over the Sweet Room, and other times when teens congregated there to make it their space. So the hostess needs to be vigilant about checking in to make sure it's a good place for the adults to gather, with occasional visits by the kids.

Numinous Beings

We've had many different Numinous Beings appear over the years. It's best to choose people to portray them who have had some performance experience or at least have a dramatic flair. Costumes are important, even if they're simple. The critical thing is that they memorize their lines. No reading from scripts, ever!

Here are some of the Numinous Beings who have graced us with their presence:

- La Befana
- A Gnome (seen above)

- Frau Holle or Holda

- Rozhanitsa

- Mother Berta and her goat Skeggi

- The Child of Wonder

- Grandfather Winter

- Saule

- The Holly King

- The Three Mothers

- Jack Frost

- Mother Star Stupendous Mermaid (a character from Kim Antieau's novel *Church of the Old Mermaids,* seen at right)

See the section on Numinous Beings for scripts and costume ideas (page 38).

the Lucy Bride

The appearance of St. Lucia and her train is the centerpiece of the evening. She gets her own section (page 45)!

Spakona: Short Tarot and Rune Readings

One year, one of the hostesses decided to be a *spakona*, or oracle-reader, for the evening. She spent most of the party in the Sweet Room doing short rune or tarot readings for the guests. They were told ahead of time (on the invitation) to be sure to bring an offering of their choice for the *spakona* if they expected a reading. This could be money, or a gift, or something to eat or drink, or even a kiss on the cheek. It was up to the *spakona* whether or not the offering was accepted.

This activity was a big hit with the guests, but the reader found that she missed most of the party. So she hasn't repeated her appearance as the *spakona*. If we wanted to do it again, I think it might be a good idea to hire someone who regularly does readings at parties, as they would not expect to participate in the party in addition to doing the readings.

Gift Exchange

On the invitation, we say "spend no more than $5." But we also say to bring a small, wrapped, *exquisite* gift. Our intention is for guests to bring really special gifts. They could be handmade, found, or recycled from personal possessions. Just don't buy junk or gag gifts. (Yes, that has happened. What a disappointment!)

Some of the best gifts have been: a hand-made calligraphy pen with a bottle of berry ink; fragrant, handmade soaps; a recycled necklace; a hand-crocheted doily or altar cloth; a mermaid ornament. Use your imagination!

Guests who are bringing a child to the party should bring a gift for that child with his or her name on the tag. The Giftbringer hands out the children's gifts first.

The Giftbringer is a different Numinous Being each year — sometimes it's the Italian witch La Befana, sometimes it's Grandfather Winter. One year it was a Gnome, once it was Lakshmi (the Hindu Goddess of Prosperity), and once it was Mother Star Stupendous Mermaid (a character from Kim Antieau's novel *Church of the Old Mermaids*). You can be wildly creative when it comes to choosing your Giftbringer!

The Giftbringer tells her or his tale and passes out the gifts to the children, calling them up one by one. Then the rest of the gifts from the gift exchange are distributed among the guests. Delighted oohs and aahs always follow the unwrapping of the gifts!

Concert

One of the high points of the evening is a mini-concert with my husband Craig Olson and others, most often our friend Julianne Marx. This is always a crowd-pleaser. The musicians have a repertoire of songs they've performed at every Lucia Party for years, and they usually sing a few new tunes too. They are sometimes joined by drummers and a bass player, and one time we had a fiddler. What would Yuletide be without great music?

In 2010, Craig and Juels released a fabulous album called *Midwinter Moon* that grew out of their performances at our Lucia Parties. The album is a collection of our favorite Yuletide songs, plus some holiday classics. You can give it a listen at: *http://midwintermoon.bandcamp.com/*.

You can watch a couple of videos from our 2009 party on YouTube, with Craig and Juels singing a song that Craig wrote called "Solstice Night," *(http://tinyurl.com/craig-juels-solsticenight)* and the classic "Baby, It's Cold Outside" *(http://tinyurl.com/craig-juels-coldoutside)*.

Sing-along Caroling

After the concert, people are often in the mood to keep on singing. We pass out songbooks of Christmas carols with alternative lyrics that we've collected over the years. Every few years, we reprint the songbooks as we often lose a few of them each year as they make their way home with guests.

We've found that it's best to include musical notation in the songbooks for new carols or ones that are not well-known. But all you need is lyrics for familiar, beloved Christmas carols. It's grand fun!

We usually sing the carols a capella, but if you have a guitarist or piano player who knows the songs well and can play accompaniment, that's even better.

Some of the alternative lyrics to traditional carols that we sing are included in the Songs section, along with the staff music for a couple of original tunes (page 58).

Plum Pudding

The presentation of a flaming plum pudding is always a grand, dramatic addition to the party. You'll need to darken the room to see it at its best; the flames are soft blue and very pretty, but hard to see unless it's dark. It's best to have two people involved: one to carry in the pudding and one to ignite and pour the brandy. We try to time the presentation with the following lines as we sing the carol "To Drive the Cold Winter Away":

Here comes the Good Dame,
Plum pudding aflame,
To drive the cold winter away!

There are a few tricks to getting the flames to ignite, which you'll find along with the recipe in the Recipes section (page 77).

Snapdragon

I learned the Victorian Christmas game of Snapdragon from my friend Waverly Fitzgerald. Like Lucia's crown of candles and the flaming plum pudding, it's yet another variation on the Midwinter theme of *lux in tenebris:* light in darkness.

Everybody loves this game — everybody! In fact, there are usually too many people gathered around the table, so they need to be encouraged to let others have a turn.

We cover an old card table with aluminum foil, which makes a nice reflective surface. It would not be a good idea to set the Snapdragon table up on a carpet or an expensive hardwood floor, as the floor can get pretty messy. A tile floor is fine, or even your outside deck or patio. I'll share Waverly's instructions and comments with you:

1. Fill a shallow heatproof bowl with raisins. Put in two or three raisins for each guest who you think will participate.

2. Warm some brandy in a pan on the stove, then pour it into the bowl, about a half inch deep.

3. Place the bowl in the middle of a table or on some other surface that can be protected from drips.

4. Turn off as many lights as possible (for dramatic effect).

5. Light the brandy on fire. The brandy will flicker with an eerie blue flame.

6. Now try to snatch the raisins out of the burning brandy and pop them into your mouth.

When you first see the flames you will be convinced this cannot be done. Once you've decided to plunge your fingers into the burning brandy, there's the shock of discovering the flames are hot (but not hot enough to burn). If you persevere and snatch out a raisin, your fingers will drip with blue flame as you fling the still-burning raisin into your mouth. It's exciting and wild and daring and noisy!*

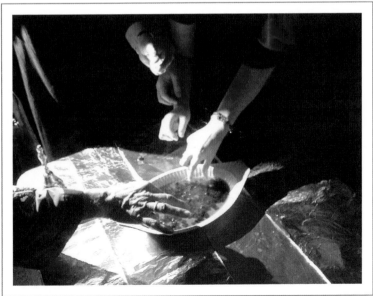

*Waverly Fitzgerald, *Celebrating Yule,* 2003, www.livinginseason.com

Drum Circle

This is a great way to end the evening on a high note. Craig brings out all his drums and percussion instruments, and other drummers have usually brought theirs as well. Sometimes there's a didgeridoo! Everyone gets into the rhythm, from young to old.

Late Night Doings

Whether or not the night ends with music or storytelling seems to depend on the talents and interests of the people who are still up and awake after most everyone has gone home. Waverly remembers this scene fondly from Helen's parties:

"By this time, the party was winding down and people were leaving, going out into the chill night for their long drives back to Seattle or Bellingham or wherever they came from. I never made it to the end since Seattle was two hours away but I was told that the evening usually ended with the reading of stories. Helen and James would gather a group in front of the wood stove and pull out one of their favorite books — Saki, for instance — and read stories. It sounded like a deliciously sleepy ending to a great party, drifting off by the fire, listening to stories at the only time of the year when stories can be told, according to many indigenous cultures."*

I remember various endings to our parties . . . sometimes there's another round of carol-singing, sometimes there's a little guitar-playing, sometimes there's just the hosts and hostesses cuddling up on the sofa. I seem to recall a group reading of Dylan Thomas's *A Child's Christmas in Wales,* and a telling of the Pacific Northwest native story of "Raven Steals the Light." I remember the hush and the sparkling colored lights and candles burning low.

We create magic for this night, then drift off to sleep still basking in its glow.

*Waverly Fitzgerald, *Celebrating Yule,* 2003, www.livinginseason.com

Sunday

On the morning after the Lucia Party, I'm usually the first one up. I make coffee and put water on for tea. Before long, our sleepy-eyed houseguests trickle out one by one, and head for the kitchen for a mug and the hot beverage of their choice. We chat, sip our tea, and nibble on leftover plum pudding, *lussekatter*, and goodies from the Sweet Room. The rest of the hostesses and their families keep arriving, until by 10 a.m. we're getting organized for Sunday brunch.

Many hands make light work! We put together a vegetable frittata, mimosas (orange juice and champagne), Wheel of the Year scones, roasted red potatoes, sausage and bacon . . . Morning tumbles into the noon hour as we relax, chat, do tarot readings, paint henna on each other, and maybe watch a DVD of Rick Steves's *European Christmas.* Mostly though, we just enjoy each other's company and take pleasure in the afterglow. By mid-afternoon those who live in Portland or Seattle or Port Townsend are on their way home. By evening, Craig and I have the house to ourselves again. We turn off all the lights except for the colored Yule lights, light the altar candles, and stoke up the fire. We snuggle on the sofa, nestling into the silence that reverberates with the sights, sounds, and feelings of the weekend just passed. The night

before, fifty-some people had celebrated here and welcomed the Return of the Light. Now, there are just the two of us.

Until, of course, next year.

Numinous Beings

You can rewrite or edit the scripts for the Numinous Beings so that they work for you and your players. Some scripts are quite short and others are lengthy. The important thing is that the lines be memorized. Nothing ruins the magic of a performance more than if the actor is reading from a script.

Costumes can be simple, but should reflect the character's age and ethnicity.

the Child of Wonder

(S/he should be played by a child, of course, dressed in white and gold.)

I am the Child of Wonder born at Winter Solstice! Yes, you know me — you have seen me in the innocent wide eyes of children. It's true that some have called me the

Christkindl, and they say that I travel through the cold, snowy night, carrying a small tree, and bringing toys and sweets to the little ones. And it's true — that's me!

When you hear the stories of "the babe wrapped in swaddling clothes, and lying in a manger," think of me.

For I am the One you see at the still point of the turning world, when Darkness gives birth to Light. My gifts to you are radiance, joy, and hope during the darkest night of the year.

A shorter version for a very young child would be something like this:

I am the Child of Wonder born at Winter Solstice! My gifts to you are joy, hope and peace on the darkest night of the year.

Fray Holda

(She should be dressed in white, with a furry coat if possible, and a crown that suggests snowflakes. If she can bring a pillowcase full of feathers, all the better. She can shake them out like the snow, and someone else can be appointed to sweep up afterward.)

I am the Old Woman of Winter — I bring the frost and the snow. When the snow begins to fall, I hear you whispering, "Old Holda is shaking her feather bed!" It is I, too, who rides the wild winds of change and forgetting. I can turn your dreams inside out or upside down. Do not fear my storms, but welcome them — for with my cleansing breath, I blow away the old year and usher in the new.

Grandfather Winter

(He should be played by an elder gentleman. He should be dressed in a red or green robe with a head wreath of greens and holly.)

You know me by many names — Grandfather Frost, Old Saint Nick, Sinterklaas, or just plain Santa. You all know me, and in your hearts you still believe, for I am the Giftbringer. And I say to you — may the New Year bring you all your hopes and dreams!

Holly King

(He should be dressed in green and wear a crown of holly — silk holly will do. He should also be holding a chalice.)

Sings: "Of all the trees that are in the wood, the holly bears the crown."

I am the Holly King, Lord of the Waning Year. You may know me as the Green Man or as the Winter King. I rule from Midsummer to Midwinter, and my reign culminates in the festivities of Yuletide. As the wren dies to make way for the robin, soon I will bow before my brother the Oak King. You will not see me again until the sun once more begins to wane. As I prepare to withdraw into the deep midwinter, I contemplate the glowing light of the reborn sun in my cup — and in this holy grail, I see visions and dreams of the year to come.

Jack Frost

Look out! Look out!
Jack Frost is about!
I'll nip at your fingers and toes;
While all through the night,
This gay little sprite
Will be working where nobody

I'll climb each tree,
Where no one will see,
My silvery powder I'll shake.
To windows I'll creep
And while you're asleep
Such wonderful pictures I'll make.

Across the grass
I will merrily pass,
And change all of its greenness to
Then home I will go
And laugh, ha, ha, ha, ho!
For what fun I have had on this night!

(Adapted by Lee LaMar from a poem by C.E. Pike. The first year that Lee played Jack Frost, he was such a big hit that the crowd insisted he do it twice!)

La Befana

(She should be dressed up as an Italian peasant, possibly with a kerchief on her head and carrying a broom as a prop. This is a longer script than most and can certainly be shortened. La Befana can be a comic figure too, so it's great if the woman playing her is good at ad-libbing. La Befana makes a great Giftbringer.)

O mio dio! These must be the coldest nights of winter — my joints are aching and my veins are full of ice water. The days are so short now you're like to miss them if you blink! And there is so much work to be done — floors to be swept, pots to be scrubbed, silver to polish, and windows to wash till they sparkle and shine! And no one to help this poor old woman with her work!

I know what they call me, those nasty children down the street —

La Strega, they call me, the neighborhood witch! Just because I am so fond of my broom! The elder ones call me *La Vecchia Donna,* Old Woman — and it's true, an older woman you won't find, not in this town.

What's that you say? Why am I busily sweeping and cleaning? Why, I am sweeping away the old year, to make room for the new . . .

Once, many years ago, I left my snug warm home on a night like this. I had been visited by three strangers in silken clothing — magicians they were, who had marked the tracks of the planets and were traveling to witness the birth of the Child of Wonder. They asked me along on their journey, knowing that I had served the Great Mother as a Maiden, and that I would know the rites to perform . . . oh but I was so busy that year! I had floors to sweep, pots to scrub, silver to polish, and windows to wash till they sparkled and shone!

I cried myself to sleep that night, remembering the promise I had made to the Great Mother in my youth, to grant each child a wish this one night a year . . . to be the Grandmother who watched over them and rewarded the worthy while chastising the naughty. They think I am leaving them gifts of candy or nuts or firecrackers, but my gifts are more potent than those: I bear the gift of talents: for art, for music, for science, for peacemaking, for the caretaking of the land.

For, you see, every child is the Holy Child, who is the Bringer of Hope and the Promise of Summer. Every child holds the future of the world in their heart and hands.

And so I travel this night of Epiphany each year on my broom, riding the winds between the worlds, gathering the offerings you make of sweet focaccia bread, and bringing gifts to the Child of Wonder: you — and you — and you.

Rozhanitsa

(She should be wearing an antler headdress. She could be carrying a torch or candle as well. If you have a white apron with red cross-stitching on it, that would be perfect!)

Look to me, my children, to keep you safe, warm, and well-fed throughout the bitter winter. For I am the oldest goddess of the Russian plains, the ancient Mother of the Deer. I ran with the herds in the Paleolithic age when the first hunter took aim. I danced through the stars too, with my sisters the Sky Deer.

I am Rozhanitsa, the Birth-Giver. At this season, I bring forth a child who is sometimes a daughter and sometimes a deer. The reindeer of the far north, you know, are the only species of deer in which the female has antlers. The folksongs say that my daughters bear golden antlers — just another way of saying they are born on the sun's birthday, don't you think?

For centuries my women have honored me by creating their rich embroidered towels, aprons, and curtains. I love the bright red threads lovingly and laboriously sewn into the crisp white linens. Yes, that's right — weave my protective magic into each stitch. I will keep your daughters safe as they labor to birth their own children. Give these cloths to each other on my birthday, December 26 — and bake the white-iced cookies I love so much, cut in the shape of a deer.

Ssssh. The night is frozen and the midnight black, but I carry my torch aloft for you, my children. I will keep you warm. I will fill your bellies. I will stay beside you till it is spring once more.

Saule

(She should be wearing yellow or gold clothing and amber necklaces, and should be carrying a basket of golden apples. One year she threw out butterscotch candies to the guests as she left — standing in for tears of amber.)*

Oh, you have risen early, my darling ones. Do you see the rosy sky beginning to brighten over the eastern hills? I am coming to you, my sweets. I am your beloved Saule, Mother Sun.

How I love to hear you sing your songs to me! Sometimes you sing that I am a red apple setting in the west. Or that I make my bed in an apple tree, where my sacred serpent, the *zaltys*, twines around my arms. In the late evening, I board my golden boat and travel beneath the world to my rising place in the east. When I am very sad, I sit in my apple orchard and weep tears of amber. But on the morning of Winter Solstice — or *Kaledos*, as we call it — I am reborn as my daughter the Morning Star, the year's young sun.

I have also heard you whisper that the magical smith Kalvis forges a goblet of gold, and that it releases me from the dark of night. I charge over the mountains of dawn in my chariot drawn by two silken horses. Oh, I do love the exhilaration of the race — just as I love my children!

I shine on all of you — there is no limit to the love I have for you. Even though you tease me when you sing: *Saule, you seem to be rushing! Go slower! Stay late in the sky! We have much work to do and need the extra light!* Oh, my dear ones! There is always tomorrow! I will rise for you again.

Dance for me on the morning of Kaledos! Sing my songs and carry the golden apples of the sun throughout the town! Greet each other with wishes of health and prosperity — on this morning, your prayers will be answered and your wishes fulfilled, Oh my beloved ones!

*Patricia Monaghan's wonderful book *O Mother Sun* (Crossing Press, 1994) is my main source of information about Saule.

Three Mothers

(One woman could be dressed in green, carrying a fir branch; one in red, carrying holly; and one in white or gold, holding a shortcake cut into eight pieces. If the three women are singers, they can also sing Helen's "Carol of the Three Mothers." See page 60 for the song.)

We are the Three Mothers, whose bounty is celebrated on Solstice Eve. We travel through the darkest night, and you may watch our night's progress as the three stars in the belt of that great figure who dominates the winter sky. We rise in the east at sunset, are overhead at midnight, and sink below the western horizon with the dawn. We are midwives to the Child of Wonder. We journey to attend the birth. We bear the gifts of our season: the never-dying branch of fir. The holly with its berry red as blood, its painful prickle like a thorn. The cakes baked in the shape of the newborn sun, incised with the mystery of Eight-in-One. Honor us by leaving us a bit of food on your table. For we are the three who turn the Wheel of the Year. Praise the sun at Midwintertide!

The Lucy Bride

The centerpiece of the evening is, of course, the arrival of the Lucy Bride with her crown of blazing candles and her tray of *lussekatter*, "light cats." These symbolize her gift of nourishment for both body and soul. Even those guests who know very little about the symbolism and history of St. Lucia are moved by the beauty of the procession. (See the Appendix on page 77 for details on why we call her the Lucy Bride, and why the pastries are called "light cats.")

At Helen's parties, the Lucy Bride and her train would start their procession outside. My friend Waverly writes in her account of the parties at Bright House: "We would see candles flickering outside the windows and hear the faint sound of female voices in song, then a rap on the door, and St. Lucia would burst in, a crown of candles flaming on her head. She would walk through the company, offering each guest one of the pastries on the tray she carried. Her female companions would sing 'Santa Lucia' and so would we all as we took our treats and thanked St. Lucia for bringing Light back to the world."*

Anna, one of the first Lucy Brides at Helen's Lucia Party, 1988

*Waverly Fitzgerald, *Celebrating Yule*, 2003, www.livinginseason.com

This is the same pattern we have followed each year at our own parties, although we have not always had big picture windows where we could watch the ladies as they made their way toward the house. And, of course, some years it rained or snowed, and this made it harder for them to walk in procession outside. The year we rented the Victorian house, the Lucy Bride descended a beautifully carved wooden staircase, and that was lovely to see. But my favorite sight is still the candles flickering outside as Lucy and her train make their way to our door. I'm so glad we have picture windows at Rainbow Cottage, where we now have the parties.

Choosing the Lucy Bride

When I hosted my first Lucia Party in 1997, I asked my friend Deb to be the Lucy Bride. I knew she could sing, and I had wonderful memories of Anna and Sandi, who both played Lucia at Helen's parties, singing the "Santa Lucia" song as they distributed the *lussekatter* to the guests.

Then the role changed hands for a few years, moving from woman to woman in our circle. It

seemed less important that the woman playing Lucia have a beautiful singing voice, and more important that she embody her otherworldly presence. Elaine made a beautiful gown the year it was her turn, and every Lucy Bride has worn it since (although we often need to alter it a bit, especially the hemline).

One year we realized that many of the young girls in our community were approaching adolescence. When one of them had her First Moon (her first menstrual period), it struck us that it would be a wonderful rite of passage to have her play the Lucy Bride. So a new tradition began: each year, Lucia is played by the girl in our community who started her moonflow since the previous Lucia Party. Of course, we don't announce this at the party. But it has become a meaningful rite of passage for them. Now the younger girls look forward to the day when they can also play the role of Lucia. If there isn't a "qualified" girl for a particular year, we ask for a volunteer among the girls and women. There's always someone who would like to portray the Lucy Bride.

Her Gown

St. Lucia is traditionally dressed in a white gown with red ribbons, but the skirt and vest we use is red, with a white blouse and petticoat underneath. The combination of red and white is important, as it symbolizes fire and light.

Elaine made the gown that we use without a pattern (she is trained in costume design). You can see it in the photo at right. It is loose enough that it can accommodate a number of different body shapes and sizes. If you do an Internet search for "lucia gown pattern" or "lucia dress pattern" you'll find a few to choose from. (Some of them are for dolls, though, and some are for clothing to wear on the island of St. Lucia.) Many of the traditional St. Lucia dresses, designed for girls to wear in church pageants, are a bit (dare I say it) dowdy. I don't think our Lucia needs to have a high neckline or a Peter Pan collar on her dress.

I love the gowns that HolyClothing.com sells, many of which would make a beautiful Lucia gown. Go to the site, click on Dresses, then search by Color: White. Choose your favorite, add a few red ribbons or a red sash and you're all set. I think the Bella style dress in white would be especially nice, and it comes in many sizes, up to 5X.

Her Crown

We always use real candles on the crown and fresh greenery. (The one notable exception was the year we rented the Victorian house and were not allowed to have burning candles.) If you go shopping in Scandinavian import stores for a crown of candles for Lucia to wear, you will find that all the crowns for sale have battery-operated candles. The reason for this is, of course, fire safety. But battery-lit Lucia crowns remind me of fireplaces with fake logs and "flames" that can be turned on with the flick of a switch. We pay a price when we value convenience and safety over the elemental nourishment of our souls. The warmth of glowing candlelight touches the human psyche in ways that electric lights never will.

Appointing two or three people to be "fire watchers" solves the issue of fire safety. Their job is to keep an eye on Lucia's lit candles and to make sure that flames are put out if hair or greenery catches on fire. We always have a fire extinguisher handy, but we've never had to use it. Women who have played the role of Lucia and worn the crown report that its weight and their awareness of the lit candles contribute to a slow, steady, queenly walk.

A few years ago we began the tradition of having Lucia wear a white lace veil under the crown. It covers her face and hair and gives her an otherworldly appearance. She is at once remote, like a goddess, and nearby, offering us her love, light, and nourishment. It's a good idea for the Lucy Bride to practice walking while she wears the veil and crown with the candles lit before the big day.

How to Make a Crown of Candles

One year Elaine and her husband Lee designed the "perfect" Lucia crown. Here's how:

1. Use copper wire that is thick enough to be sturdy but flexible enough to bend.

2. Make the base by creating a circle of wire measured to the size of the head of the woman playing the Lucy Bride. Use one continuous strand of wire and wrap it around her head five or six times.

3. Cut four individual pieces of wire about ten inches in length. Wrap them around the candles that will be used on the crown, for a perfect fit. The "holders" should be about two inches deep so the candles can't fall out. The candles should be at least eight inches long — if they are shorter, you may need the fire extinguisher! Dripless utility candles work well. We have five candles on our crown, though some Lucia

crowns have seven or even nine candles. All are mystic numbers, but we have found that five candles, one for each of the four directions plus the center of the sacred circle, work quite well.

4. Secure the candleholders to the base of the crown with more copper wire. The base of the crown is now done, and can be reused every year. (You could also add padding of some kind under it, to make it feel softer.)

5. On the day of the party, cut fresh greenery for the crown. Lingonberry and whortleberry are the traditional greens for Lucia's crown, but we always use the greens we find in our own back yards. For us, that's cedar, fir, and always, of course, holly. (We also like to add a little sage, for wisdom.) Weave the greens into the strands of the copper base and secure them with florist's wire. Add red and white ribbons (symbols of fire and light) if you like. Use new white candles in the crown every year, as they are symbolic of the new year that is born at Winter Solstice.

Making the Lussekatter

The *lussekatter* are traditional saffron-flavored rolls served by St. Lucia. The word means "Lucy cats" or "light cats," most likely a reference to the magical cats who pulled the goddess Freya's chariot through the sky. They are usually formed in an X, the shape of the rune *gefjon*, the Giver, one of the names of Freya. When the ends of the X are curled under in a clockwise direction, the shape is that of an ancient sun symbol. You will also see traditional *lussekatter* in an S shape, like the rune *soweilo*, or *sigel*, the sun.

The rolls are easy to make, but the process is time consuming, like baking bread. The woman or girl who is going to play the Lucy Bride is usually the one who makes the rolls. It's a nice thing for mother and daughter to do together. They can say prayers and blessings as the dough is kneaded. This will, of course, make the gifts of the Goddess even more magical. The Lucy Bride should know that the saffron turns the dough a light yellow, the color of the newborn sun, and the raisins symbolize the eyes of Freya's "cats of light."

See the Recipes section for instructions on how to make the *lussekatter* (page 78).

The Train

The Lucy Bride is followed by her train, usually three to five girls or women. If there are more than that, it's hard for them to make their way through the crowded rooms.

Each girl should wear a cape or cloak and carry a lit taper in a candle holder. The old-fashioned brass "chamber candlesticks" with a finger ring work great and look good too. One year we bought hurricane glasses to place over the candles to keep them from blowing out as it was windy outside.

It's best to decide ahead of time who will be in the train, as there are often too many volunteers at the last moment and a limited number of cloaks. It's important for their modern clothes to be covered up to maintain the sense of mystery. They should already know the song "Santa Lucia." Memorizing the lyrics is always best.

I love beeswax candles and buy mine every year from Blue Corn Naturals (www.beeswaxcandles.com).

Getting Ready

After dinner is over, it's time for the girl playing the Lucy Bride to undergo her transformation and get dressed in Lucy's gown. Usually her mom helps her with this, and the girls in the train come too. It's important to designate a dressing room that's located in a place where they can slip outside without being seen by most of the party guests. In our house, the laundry room, which is located near the back door, serves this purpose very well.

the Invocation

After the Lucy Bride is dressed and the crown settled on her head, we ask the girls to be quiet for a few minutes while one of the elder women invokes the spirit of St. Lucia into the Lucy Bride. This can be as simple as opening up your heart, and murmuring words like these:

"Santa Lucia, you whom we know as Juno Lucina, Freya, and Brigit, the maiden and mother who bring us the Light . . . Come into our daughter, our sister, tonight. Fill her with your radiance and your grace. May all those who see her tonight be blessed by you. May all those who partake of the *lussekatter* be nourished and filled. Blessed be."

Then the crown of candles is lit and we begin.

the Procession

The outdoor path should be lit with rope lights or luminarias, so the girls do not stumble or trip. If it's icy outside, the host will have sanded the pathway, steps, and porch.

The girls should walk slowly, with Lucy in the lead, and be softly singing "Santa Lucia." As they approach the doorway to the house, the assembled guests are usually already singing the song themselves and someone has dimmed the lights. The Lucy Bride approaches each and every person in the house and offers them a pastry and a silent blessing as the guests continue to sing. After making sure that no one has been missed, she and her train leave by another door and vanish into the night.

The Song: "Santa Lucia"

We sing the traditional Italian melody and lyrics, but there are alternative lyrics you can sing as well (see page 53 in the Songs section).

Night plods with heavy tread
Court and cot cov'ring,
O'er earth, now sunshine's sped,
Shadows are hov'ring.
Mirk in our home takes flight
When comes with tapers bright,
Santa Lucia, Santa Lucia.

2.
Mute was the night with gloom;
Now hear faint bustling
In every silent room
Like pinions rustling.

Lo! On our threshold there
White-clad, with flame-crowned hair
Santa Lucia, Santa Lucia.

3.
"Dark soon swift wing shall take
From Earth's vales darkened."
We to the words she spake
In wonder hearken'd.
"Now shall another morn
From rosy skies be born."
Santa Lucia, Santa Lucia.

You can see a video of the procession of our 2009 Lucy Bride here: *http://tinyurl.com/lucia-bride-2009*

Some Lucy Brides Speak . . .

Each woman or girl who embodies Lucia at a party or in a ceremony has experienced the love and blessing of the goddess/saint moving through her. Elaine told me "it was like I was in another world. Once I put the veil on, it was no longer just me. I definitely felt Her presence. Once I stepped into the circle, it was like She just slipped into my body and I was Lucia. It was a very intense experience and a little difficult to explain."

Betsy agrees: "The experience was just beautiful. I felt so full of love and blessing, and I just had to touch people to let them know and feel the blessings coming through me. I felt new and young, and like the 'white' bride I never got to be. I could feel the darkness scatter when I came into the room. Everyone singing the Santa Lucia song made my head spin with hope, joy, and love. I would do it again anytime, since it was very helpful in what is usually a very sad time of year for me."

One of our younger Lucy Brides, Steph, had this to say about her experience: "Being a Lucy Bride is about understanding Lucia and what her purpose was: to bring light and to help sustain life. When I was getting ready to be St. Lucia, I was concerned about tripping in the dress, the weight of the crown on my head, and the hot wax from the candles. But the second that I went into the house, all of those thoughts that had been so important went away. They became so very insignificant compared to being absolutely filled with an abundance of kindness at that moment. It wasn't about me anymore. It was about honoring Lucia who came from a place of kindness. My concerns about my costume and hot wax turned into being concerned with whether or not there would be enough 'Lucy cats' to go around."

Decorations

We always gather fresh greenery for the doorways, tables, and windowsills, and wrap it around stairway banisters. There's nothing like filling the house with the scent of freshly cut cedar and fir. We gather holly and herbs too — anything we can find that's evergreen and in season. There are always several hostesses and guests who live in the woods and have access to plenty of cedar, hemlock, and fir.

We also take down some of the artwork that usually hangs on our walls and replace it with images of numinous beings, like Lucia and the Holly King.

Christmas and Solstice books make great decorations too. And . . . we collect Lucia paraphernalia! You can find lovely things (and some cheesy stuff as well) at Scandinavian import shops like the online Ingebretsens.com.

See the next page for some of my favorite Lucia "stuff"!

I found the Lucia figurine at right in a gift shop in southern California over twenty years ago. The coffee pot had broken off the tray, so I asked the store owner how much she wanted for it "as is." (It normally sold for $50.) She must have had the holiday spirit that day, because she gave it to me! We've displayed it every year since then.

Here are some Lucia mobiles, prints, ornaments, and tiles. I found most of these online by searching for Scandinavian or Swedish imports or gifts. After clicking through to a store like Ingebretsen's, I search for "Christmas" or "Lucia" and see what I can find. You can also look on eBay. And of course if you have a Scandinavian import shop in your town, that's always a good place to look for Lucia decorations, especially around the holidays.

Fresh greenery, sparkling silver, and candles everywhere are really all you need . . .

One year I found the beautiful St. Lucia figurine below on eBay, but I haven't been able to find a supplier for her since. She makes a perfect centerpiece for the Yuletide altar. (There's another photo of her on page 13.)

There used to be an "American Girl" doll called Kirsten

and you could buy a St. Lucia outfit for her (shown at left). She made a great decoration for the party too. The company retired her at the end of 2009, but you can still find her online if you search.

Songs

What would the Yuletide be without its enchanting music? We are blessed to have wonderful musicians in our community, and I bet you do too.

Over the years, we've collected alternative lyrics to familiar, beloved Christmas carols, and I've included some of those here. I've also included the staff music and lyrics to an original song by Helen Farias, "Rozhanitsa," and one by Craig Olson, "Solstice Night." These are two of my favorite Yuletide songs.

Both of them, plus most of the other songs I'm sharing with you in this section, are on the album *Midwinter Moon*.

We have about forty copies of our songbooks that we pass out during the party so that everyone can sing along. The songs in this section should be a good start for you to create a songbook of your own. Visit the Lucia Party secret website for links to sources for more alternative lyrics.

Let's start with the night's anthem, "Santa Lucia" (staff music and lyrics are on the next page). Most people have heard this song, but if you haven't, just go to iTunes and search for it. You'll find versions by everyone from Enrico Caruso to Elvis Presley.

Santa Lucia

Although many new songs are still being written for St. Lucia processions in Sweden, this one, with its familiar, haunting melody, is our favorite. The lyrics are a bit awkward, but they seem to add to the "antique" feeling of the experience. At our parties the women and girls in Lucia's train sing this song and as they enter the room where the party guests are assembled, everyone joins in. It is always a moment of sheer loveliness and grace.

Melody: Traditional Neapolitan

Lyrics: Arvid Rosen, 1928

1.
Night plods with heavy tread
Court and cot cov'ring,
O'er earth, now sunshine's sped,
Shadows are hov'ring.
Mirk in our home takes flight
When comes with tapers bright,
Santa Lucia, Santa Lucia.

2.
Mute was the night with gloom;
Now hear faint bustling
In every silent room
Like pinions rustling.
Lo! On our threshold there
White-clad, with flame-crowned hair
Santa Lucia, Santa Lucia.

3.
"Dark soon swift wing shall take
From Earth's vales darkened."
We to the words she spake
In wonder hearken'd.
"Now shall another morn
From rosy skies be born."
Santa Lucia, Santa Lucia.

***Alternative Lyrics** by Shaw Fitzgerald, age 12:*
Darkness is at its peak
But light is on its way
Springtime is coming soon
Winter will fade away
She brings light to our house
She brings joy to our lives
Santa Lucia, Santa Lucia

Alternative Lyrics for "Santa Lucia"

(Attributed to the Greenwood Singers, 1992)

1.

Santa Lucia
Thy light is glowing
Through darkest winter night
Comfort bestowing
Dreams for the future bright
Come in the morning light
Santa Lucia, Santa Lucia

2.

Through silent winter gloom
Thy song come winging
To waken earth anew
Glad carols bringing
Come now, O Queen of Light
Wearing thy crown so bright
Santa Lucia, Santa Lucia

3.

Santa Lucia
Yuletide foretelling
Fill hearts with hope and cheer
Dark fears dispelling
Bring to the world again
Peace and good will to men
Santa Lucia, Santa Lucia

Lady Greensleeves

Melody: "Greensleeves" or "What Child Is This?" Lyrics by Lady Isadora

1.

Midwinter Moon is shining bright
The Yuletide log is burning
Good people gather round tonight
The Sabbat Wheel is turning.
Joy, mirth, the Sun's rebirth
Now as of old we greet thee
Gladdening the songs we sing
Of praises to the Lady.

2.

'Twas at the feast of bright Beltane
When we were all a-Maying
Sweet minstrel queen in her gown of green
Spring roundelay was playing.

And though now robed in snow
Her wintry garb deceives
For bedecked with holly and mistletoe
She is still our Lady Greensleeves.

3.

So drink ye wassail everyone
Good pagans all make merry
With wine as red as the reborn Sun
As red as holly berry.
Dance, sing, come join the ring
As her Yuletide spell she weaves
Fair Queen the Evergreen
Sweet lovely Lady Greensleeves.

Solstice Night

Craig wrote this song for the first Lucia Party we hosted in 1997. It was such a crowd-pleaser that a sing-along has become a Lucia Party tradition. Craig finally recorded a rockin' version of it in 2010 for the album *Midwinter Moon*.

Music & Lyrics by Craig Olson

1.

We gather on this sacred eve,
the Yuletide log is burning.
Tribe and family join as one,
the Wheel of Life is turning.

2.

We celebrate the sun's rebirth,
From darkness he is growing.
Bringing warmth to frozen lands,
And set our hearts to glowing.

(CHORUS)
Sing, ye, of the mystery,
Buried in the ground.
The longest night of all the year,
'Tis there our hope is found.

3.

As winter holds us in her arms,
The frozen wren is flying.
Oaken traveler comes again,
The Holly King is dying.

(CHORUS)

4.

As we depart our separate ways,
Through fields afar go roaming.
Remembering on Solstice night,
As day returns from gloaming.

(CHORUS)

In the Bleak Midwinter

This has long been one of my favorite Yuletide carols, and I love Craig's revised lyrics. Here is a slideshow/video "Christmas card" I put together in 2008, set to this tune: *http://tinyurl.com/lucia-bleak-midwinter.*

Music by Gustav Holst, 1874-1934. Orignal text by Christina Rossetti, 1830-1894.
Revised lyrics by Craig Olson

In the bleak midwinter, frosty wind made moan,
Earth stood hard as iron, water like a stone.
Snow had fallen, snow on snow, snow on snow,
In the bleak midwinter, long ago.

Darkness cannot hold you, nor your sorrows keep,
All the earth awakens from this winter's sleep.
In the bleak midwinter a stable place shall be,
Filled with home and harvest, blessed family.

Lovers, friends and dreamers, we are gathered here,
Candles on this darkest night of the year.
Still our Mother only, in her earthly bliss,
Holds Her dear beloved, softly with a kiss.

What then shall I give Her, poor as I am?
If I were a shepherd, I would bring a lamb;
And if I were a Wise One, I would do my part,
Yet what I can I'll give Her, I will give my heart.

Rozhanitsa

I first learned this song in the early 1990s from my friend Helen, who wrote it in honor of the Russian Winter Goddess Rozhanitsa. (We often honor Her as one of the Numin-ous Beings at our parties too; see page 36.)

"One year in the fall while reading about Rozhanitsa, I was visited by a song, complete with lyrics," Helen wrote in 1992. "It sounds like an old Russian folksong, and I've been plagued by the concern that I may be unconsciously plagiarizing an anonymous Russian. But I know the words came through me, and probably the music too, because after the first rush, I had to work at it and perfect it. I see this Goddess in the spare winter landscape, and most especially in the constellation we call Orion, whom I feel certain was one source of the people's sense of Her presence throughout the long, dark season, be She called Rozhanitsa, Freya, Brigit, or something else."*

I have a wonderful memory of singing this haunting melody with Helen and other circle sisters during an ice storm many winters ago when we did, indeed, wonder if we would ever see Spring again.

Music & Lyrics by Helen Farias

1.
Rozhanitsa of the snows,
Rozhanitsa of the barren trees,
Rozhanitsa of the hungry birds,
Come near our fire.

2.
When the killing blizzard blows,
When the berries on the bushes freeze,
Rozhanitsa, hear our tender words,
Come near our fire.
Stay by us 'til Spring breaks through.

3.
Little Mother of the deer,
Little Mother of the winter sun,
Little Mother of the starry night,
Come near our fire.

4.
When the fields are bleak and sere,
When the icy streams forget to run,
Rozhanitsa, hold aloft your light,
Come near our fire.
Stay by us 'til Spring breaks through.

*Helen Farias, "Festal Songs: Rozhanitsa," *The Beltane Papers' Octava*, Samhain 1992.

to Drive the Cold Winter Away

Helen had a knack for revising lyrics to beloved melodies. I first heard this song from her before Loreena McKennitt recorded her own well-known version. It's one of the most beautiful Yule carols ever written.

Music: "In Praise of Christmas," England, 17th century. Lyrics by Helen Farias.

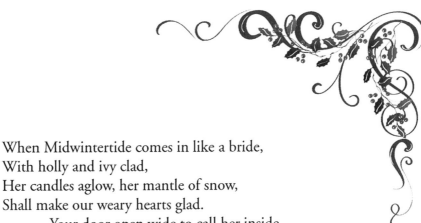

When Midwintertide comes in like a bride,
With holly and ivy clad,
Her candles aglow, her mantle of snow,
Shall make our weary hearts glad.
>   Your door open wide to call her inside
>   To brighten the gloomy day.
>   Our wassail is blest, our carols are best
>   To drive the cold winter away.

This time of the year is spent in good cheer
And friends together do meet
To sit by the fire, with magic conspire
To make their holidays sweet.
>   The Lady and Lord with circle and ward
>   Will bid the good spirits stay,
>   And at our behest they'll banish the rest
>   To drive the cold winter away.

So these are the days we joyfully praise,
Despite the darkening year.
We trust that the Light that shines in the night
Dispels all sorrow and fear.
>   The stars in the sky that sparkle on high
>   Will render the long night gay.
>   Here comes the Good Dame, plum pudding aflame
>   To drive the cold winter away.

Carol of the Three Mothers

Music: "Let All Mortal Flesh Keep Silent," France, 16th century. Lyrics by Helen Farias.*

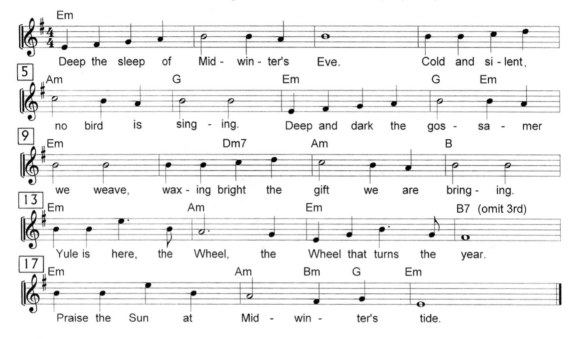

1. All
Deep the sleep of Midwinter's Eve;
Cold and silent, no bird is singing.
Deep and dark the gossamer we weave,
Waxing bright the gift we are bringing.
> Yule is here, the Wheel,
> The Wheel that turns the year.
> Praise the Sun at Midwintertide!

2. First Mother
Green and verdant, white against the snow
Never dying, ever-living bough:
This my Gift, that every child may know
Life returns, though earth is sleeping now.
> Yule is here, the Wheel,
> The Wheel that turns the year.
> Praise the Sun Queen awesome and mild.

3. Second Mother
Red as lifeblood, bright against the snow,
Ember-brilliant berries, winter's flame:
These my Gift, that every child may know
Life still burns within the earth's cold frame.
> Yule is here, the Wheel,
> The Wheel that turns the year.
> Sing Her praises, sing far and wide.

4. Third Mother
Gold and silver-white upon the snow,
Bright the Sun who rises in the east:
This my Gift, that every child may know
Seasons turn — tonight is Winter's feast.
> Yule is here, the Wheel,
> The Wheel that turns the year.
> Sing the Sun Maid, Lucia Bride!

5. All
Sisters, brothers all, receive your choice,
Take our gift, the web of Eight-in-One.
Sing, be hopeful, revel and rejoice
In the circling dance of the Sun.
> Yule is here, the Wheel,
> The Wheel that turns the year.
> Praise the Mother, praise the Child!

*Helen Farias, "Carol of the Three Mothers," *The Beltane Papers' Octava*, Yule 1985.

Menus & Recipes

The food is, of course, one of the main delights of the Lucia Party. In fact, some have said that it is our religious duty to feast as much as possible on St. Lucia's Day in order to assure plenty for the rest of the year! So this is a time to eat all you like, guilt-free.

I've included sample menus and recipes for some of our favorite dishes. We've tried different themes over the years, like an emphasis on Scandinavian food or encouraging guests to bring foods from their own ancestral traditions. But these are the dishes that we like the best. We are blessed to have so many great cooks in our community! The hosts and host-esses provide the main courses (as well as many other dishes) and guests are asked to bring a side dish, a beverage, and a sweet for the Sweet Room. We do our best to have a wide range of vegetarian, vegan, and gluten-free dishes in addition to food for the omnivores. No one leaves hungry.

Appetizers

Artichoke Dip
Popcorn
Bruschetta
Cheese and Crackers
Deviled Eggs
Mixed Nuts

Drinks

Farm Fresh Apple Cider
*Eggnog (two kinds, with and
          without alcohol)
Wine, Beer, Mead . . .
Raspberry and Blackberry Cordial
         made last summer
Lucy Juice
Amaretto, Irish Cream,
         Peppermint Schnapps & Cocoa
Coffee, Tea, and Water

*Recipe included in the following pages

Dinner Menu

Roast Turkey
Spiral Ham
*Baked Salmon
*Swedish Meatballs with Noodles
*Elaine's To-Die-For Mac & Cheese
*Roasted Roots
Au Gratin Potatoes
Mashed Potatoes w/Gravy
Quiche (Vegetarian)
Tomato Tarts

Lots of Green Salad
*Wild Rice Salad with Cranberries
    and Pecans
*Beet Salad with Apples
Green Beans
Beets (Pickled, Roasted, etc)
Beet Salmon Salad
Roasted Brussel Sprouts
A Variety of Pasta and Grain Dishes
*Blue Cornbread

Sweet Room Favorites

*Plum Pudding
*Frangos
Peppermint Bark
*Gingersnaps
*Danish Pastry
Michael's Baklava

Pumpkin Pie
*Apple Pear Crisp
Thirteen Kinds of Cookies
Truffles
Toffee

Menu for Sunday Brunch

*Vegetable Frittata
Roasted Fingerling Potatoes
Bacon, Ham, and/or Sausage
*Wheel of the Year Scones
Leftover Treats from the Sweet Room
Leftover Lussekatter
Blueberry Pancakes
Fruit Salad
Salad Greens
Mimosas (Orange Juice and Champagne)
Coffee and Tea

*Recipe included in the following pages

Recipes: Main Dishes

Baked Salmon

Salmon is a must for those of us in the Pacific Northwest; it's one of our sacred foods. We always buy wild-caught salmon, never farmed!

INGREDIENTS

> 2–4 cloves minced garlic
> 1/2 sliced onion
> 6 tablespoons extra-virgin olive oil
> 1 teaspoon dill weed
> 1 teaspoon salt
> 1/2 teaspoon freshly ground black pepper
> 1/2 lemon, sliced thin
> Juice of 1/2 lemon
> 1 tablespoon fresh chopped parsley
> 1/4 stick butter
> 1 large fillet wild-caught salmon

DIRECTIONS

1. Prepare marinade in a glass bowl by mixing garlic, olive oil, dill, salt, pepper, lemon juice and parsley. Place salmon fillet in a glass baking dish, and cover with the marinade. Marinate in the refrigerator about 1 hour, turning occasionally. (Don't marinade more than one hour.)

2. Preheat oven to 375° F.

3. Place fillet in aluminum foil, cover with marinade, pats of butter, onion, and lemon slices, and seal. Place sealed salmon in the glass dish, and bake 15 to 20 minutes. Thicker pieces of fish will take a little longer.

— *Craig Olson*

Swedish Meatballs

INGREDIENTS

2 slices fresh white bread
1/4 cup milk
3 tbs butter, divided
1/2 cup finely chopped onion
A pinch plus 1 teaspoon salt
3/4 pound ground beef
3/4 pound ground pork
2 large egg yolks
1/2 teaspoon black pepper
1/4 teaspoon ground allspice
1/4 teaspoon freshly grated nutmeg
1/4 cup flour (unbleached white)
3 cups beef broth
1/4 cup heavy cream

DIRECTIONS

1. Preheat oven to 200° F.

2. Tear the bread into pieces and place in a small mixing bowl along with the milk. Set aside.

3. In a 12-inch straight-sided sauté pan or skillet, melt 1 tablespoon of the butter over medium heat. Add the onion and a pinch of salt, and sweat until the onions are soft. Remove from the heat and set aside.

4. Combine the bread and milk mixture, ground beef, pork, egg yolks, 1 teaspoon of kosher salt, black pepper, allspice, nutmeg, and onions. Mix until thoroughly combined.

5. Shape into rounds the size of golf balls, trying to make them uniform in size.

6. Heat the remaining butter in the sauté pan or skillet over medium-low heat. Add the meatballs and sauté until golden brown on all sides, about 7 to 10 minutes. Remove the meatballs and put them in an ovenproof dish using a slotted spoon. Place in the warmed oven.

7. Once all of the meatballs are cooked, decrease the heat to low and add the flour to the pan or skillet. Whisk until lightly browned, approximately 1 to 2 minutes. Gradually add the beef stock and whisk until sauce begins to thicken. Add the cream and continue to cook until the gravy reaches the desired consistency. Remove the meatballs from the oven, cover with the gravy and serve over noodles.

— Elaine Nichols

Elaine's to-Die-For Mac & Cheese

INGREDIENTS

1 pound elbow macaroni (gluten-free, if you prefer)
1/2 cup plus 1 tablespoon butter
2 cups shredded cheese (whatever you have on hand: cheddar, jack, muenster)
1/2 cup shredded smoked gouda cheese
1 cup fontina cheese
2 cups half & half
2 large eggs, lightly beaten
1/4 teaspoon salt or Herbamare
1/8 teaspoon black pepper, freshly ground

DIRECTIONS

1. Preheat oven to 350°. Lightly butter a deep 2 1/2 quart casserole dish. Bring a large pot of salted water to a boil over high heat, add the elbow macaroni and cook until just tender (about 7 minutes). Do not overcook. Drain and return to the pot.

2. In a small saucepan, melt 1/2 cup butter, pour over macaroni and stir. In a large bowl, mix the cheese. To the macaroni, add the half & half, 3 cups of the shredded cheese and the eggs. Season with salt or Herbamare and pepper. Transfer to the buttered casserole dish. Sprinkle with the remaining 1/2 cup of cheese and dot with the remaining butter.

3. Bake until it is bubbling around the edges, about 35 minutes. Serve hot.

— Elaine Nichols

Recipes: Side Dishes

Roasted Roots

INGREDIENTS

4 to 6 Carrots
Potatoes (reds or Yukon golds are preferred)
Sweet potato
Yam
Large beet

Vegan

Large onion
Garlic
Turnip
Rutabaga

DIRECTIONS

1. Chop root vegetables into one to two inch cubes, mix them all together and place in an unoiled casserole baking dish.

2. Cover and bake at 350° for 35 minutes. Check to see if they are soft. You can uncover and brown them at the same heat for five to ten minutes more, and serve.

Variations: Sprinkle with olive oil, salt, rosemary, and thyme; add unpeeled garlic cloves during the last 20 minutes.

— *Nora Cedarwind Young*

Beet Salad with Apples

INGREDIENTS

1 pound pickled sliced beets
2 medium tart apples
2 tablespoons mayonnaise

Vegetarian

1 tablespoon sugar
1/8 teaspoon salt
Freshly ground pepper
2 tablespoons chopped parsley

DIRECTIONS

1. Drain beets and cut into strips 1/4 inch thick.

2. Peel apples and dice finely.

3. Mix beets, apples, mayonnaise, and sugar, salt, and pepper to taste.

4. Toss ingredients lightly together. Garnish with chopped parsley.

— *Debra Strom*

Wild Rice Salad with Cranberries and Pecans

INGREDIENTS

Vegetarian

1 cup wild rice
3 cups water
1/2 tsp salt
1 tablespoon butter
1/2 cup dried cranberries
1/2 cup chopped toasted pecans

1/4 cup sliced green onions
1 tablespoon lemon juice
2 tablespoon olive oil
½ teaspoon sugar
1 teaspoon grated orange peel
Salt and freshly ground pepper

DIRECTIONS

1. Bring rice, 1/2 teaspoon salt, butter, and water to a boil. Reduce heat to low, cover and cook for 50 minutes. Do not stir. Do not uncover. Remove from stove and let sit, covered, for 10 minutes. Then uncover, fluff up with a fork, and let cool to almost room temperature.

2. Mix the rice, cranberries, pecans, and green onions together in a medium sized serving bowl.

3. Dressing: In a jar, mix the lemon juice, olive oil, orange peel, and sugar. Add salt and pepper to taste. Just before serving, mix the dressing in with the rice mixture. Serve warm, chilled, or room temperature.

— *Elaine Nichols*

Blue Cornbread

INGREDIENTS

1 cup blue corn meal
1/2 cup whole wheat flour
1/2 cup unbleached pastry flour
2 teaspoons baking powder

1/2 teaspoon salt
1 egg
1/2 cup honey
1/4 cup sunflower oil
3 cups buttermilk

DIRECTIONS

1. Combine dry ingredients. Combine wet ingredients. Mix the two together. The batter will be quite watery.

2. Pour into greased 9x9 pan. Bake for 50 minutes at 350° or until top is springy when gently touched. Makes three layers, the middle is a custard (so don't worry if it's moist; it's supposed to be).

— *Michele Morrissey (adapted from the Tassajara Bread Book)*

Recipes: Sweets

Danish Pastry

PASTRY
1 cup flour
1/2 cup butter
2 tablespoon water

TOPPING
1/2 cup butter
1 cup water
1 teaspoon
    almond extract
1 cup flour • 3 eggs

ICING
1 1/2 cups powdered sugar
2 tablespoons butter
1/2 teaspoon vanilla
1-2 teaspoon milk

WALNUTS

DIRECTIONS

1. Heat oven to 350° F. Place 1 cup flour in medium bowl. Cut in 1/2 cup softened butter, using pastry blender or your hands. Sprinkle 2 tablespoons water over mixture; toss with fork.

2. Gather pastry into a ball; divide in half. Pat each half into a 12x3-inch rectangle, about 3 inches apart on ungreased cookie sheet.

3. In a 2–quart saucepan, heat 1/2 cup butter and 1 cup water to a rolling boil; remove from heat. Quickly stir in almond extract and 1 cup flour. Stir vigorously over low heat about 1 minute or until mixture forms a ball. Remove from heat. Add eggs; beat until smooth. Spread half of the topping over each rectangle.

4. Bake about 1 hour or until topping is crisp and brown; remove from pan to cooling rack. Cool completely.

5. In medium bowl, mix the powdered sugar, butter, vanilla and milk. Spread over pastry and sprinkle with nuts sliced crosswise. My mother used to slice maraschino cherries and make flower shapes on top along with the walnuts. Although it was pretty, I don't do this as I don't like maraschino cherries.

— *Elaine Nichols*

Frangos: Chocolate Peppermint Cream Candies

INGREDIENTS

1 cup butter
2 cups powdered sugar
16 oz. semi-sweet chocolate, melted
4 eggs
1 teaspoon peppermint extract
2 teaspoon vanilla
2 cups crushed graham cracker crumbs (or crushed gluten-free shortbread cookie crumbs)
Garnish: maraschino cherries

DIRECTIONS

1. Cream butter and sugar. Add melted chocolate. Beat until mixed well. Beat in eggs while the mixture is still hot. Add peppermint and vanilla flavorings and blend well.

2. Use small foil cups used in candy-making. Sprinkle bottom of each cup liner with crushed cracker or cookie crumbs. Spoon in chocolate mixture. Sprinkle additional crumbs (or crushed peppermint sticks) on top. Place in freezer until firm. Garnish each one with a maraschino cherry.

These are oh-so-rich! A little bit goes a long, long way. It's not something you eat every day, but so nice to have a bite during the holidays.

— *Joanna Powell Colbert*

Apple Pear Crisp

INGREDIENTS

Mix of apples and pears, peeled and sliced
1 cup sugar
1/4 cup arrowroot powder
2 tablespoons finely ground brown rice flour
1 teaspoon cinnamon

Combine the apples and pears with mixture of sugar, arrowroot powder, flour, cinnamon. Place in pie tin.

Gluten-free, Vegan

TOPPING

1/2 cup brown rice flour
1 cup gluten-free oats
2 cups pecans, toasted
2 tsp. cinnamon
1 cup brown sugar

1/2 cup coconut oil, melted

Combine the topping ingredients and spread over top. Pour coconut oil on top evenly. Cook until apples are soft and top is cooked, about 45 minutes.

— *Elaine Nichols*

Gingersnaps

I love these because they have three kinds of ginger in them! (For a gluten-free version, you can use Pamela's Baking Mix and omit the baking soda.)

INGREDIENTS

1 cup tightly packed dark brown sugar
2/3 cup coconut oil (liquid)
1/4 cup molasses
1 egg
2 1/4 cups all-purpose flour
2 teaspoon ground ginger
2 tablespoon baking soda
1/2 teaspoon salt
1 1/2 tablespoon finely chopped fresh ginger
1/2 cup finely chopped crystallized ginger

DIRECTIONS

1. In a large mixing bowl, mix the sugar and oil. Add the molasses and egg and beat well.

2. Stir in the flour, ground ginger, baking soda, and salt until well blended. Add the fresh and crystallized ginger and mix well.

3. Cover the bowl and refrigerate for at least two hours or overnight.

4. Preheat the over to 300° F. Spray or wipe a baking sheet with vegetable oil.

5. Shape the dough into 1/2-inch balls and place on the sheet about 2 inches apart. You can also roll the dough out to 1/4 inch thickness, and cut it into shapes with cookie cutters.

6. Bake for 8–10 minutes or until crisp; remove from the oven and cool on a wire rack.

— *Joanna Powell Colbert*

Plum Pudding

INGREDIENTS

1 cup butter • 2 cups sugar • 12 eggs
1 cup hazelnuts or pecans, coarsely chopped
1 cup dried or candied fruit
4 cups fine dried bread or cake crumbs
    (any non-savory bread will do)
4 teaspoons cinnamon
½ teaspoon cloves
1 teaspoon allspice

DIRECTIONS

1. Preheat oven to 375° F.

2. Grease a decorative bundt pan. Dust the pan with fine dried bread or cake crumbs.

3. Cream butter and sugar until very light, with a fluffy texture. It should be full of air.

4. Beat in the eggs, one at a time.

5. Sprinkle the nuts and fruit with a little flour. Stir into the batter.

6. Combine crumbs and spices. Add to batter.   7. Pour into prepared bundt pan.

8. Bake at 375° for at least 40 minutes. Check to see if it's done by inserting a toothpick, which should come out clean. Cake should be lightly brown on top and pulling away from pan edges. Cool on a rack for 10 minutes in the pan, then invert and remove pan. Cool completely before placing on a "presentation" plate.

PRESENTATION OF THE FLAMING PUDDING

(Two people is best for this. One carries the cake, the other ignites and pours the brandy.) Cake must be at room temperature (not chilled). The presentation plate should have a good rim to keep flaming brandy from spilling on the floor, your clothes, etc. Just before the presentation, gently warm the brandy in a small pan. Note: prolonged heating will drive off the alcohol and the cake won't flame.

Cue the music if using. Darken room. The flames are a soft blue and very pretty, but hard to see if room isn't dark. Ignite brandy – use a long match rather than a lighter to save your fingers. Enter the party room to applause!

— *Sharon Lawrence, adapted from a recipe in The Joy of Cooking*

Lussekatter

There are many variations on this recipe. If your budget is tight, you might want to cut back on the amount of saffron. It is quite expensive and it does affect the taste of the rolls. *Lussekatter* is good with or without the spices, but is best when the exact amounts in the recipe are used. You'll want to make as many rolls as there are guests at your party, with a few

INGREDIENTS

1/4 cup warm water
1 envelope active dry yeast (fresh)
1 cup milk
1/3 cup butter
2/3 cup sugar
1/4 teaspoon salt
1 egg
1/4 teaspoon powdered saffron
1 cardamom seed, crushed
    or 1/8 teaspoon powdered cardamom)
4 1/4 cups (about) all-purpose flour
Raisins (golden ones are especially nice)
1 egg, beaten

DIRECTIONS

1. Blend water and yeast in large mixing bowl.

2. Bring milk almost to a boil and add butter; stir in sugar and salt.

3. Cool mixture to lukewarm. Add to yeast mixture and stir in 1 egg, saffron, and cardamom.

4. Stir in flour gradually and beat thoroughly.

5. Place dough in a greased bowl; cover and set in a warm place to rise until double in bulk. Knead on a floured board for 2 minutes and roll out in small portions.

6. Cut into strips about 5 by 1/2 inches. Take two strips and place in the shape of the letter X, curling in the ends. Add 4 raisins in the center of the bun, or one at each curled end.

7. Place on greased baking sheet; cover and let rise for 1 hour.

8. Brush with 1 beaten egg, then bake at 400 degrees for 12 minutes or until evenly browned.

— Helen Farias,"Festal Foods," The Beltane Papers' Octava, 1988

Recipes: Drinks

Eggnog

If the only kind of eggnog you've ever tasted is the kind you buy at the supermarket in a plastic carton, you owe it to yourself to try the real thing. Be sure you buy your eggs from a local, trusted supplier.

This should be made about a week before the party to allow it to mellow. You can also make a non-alcoholic version for the kids and those who prefer not to drink alcohol. This batch serves 30. We bring it out after dinner and fill a punch bowl with it. Each punch bowl has a card that says "With Alcohol" or "Without Alcohol." Do I need to mention that the version with alcohol packs quite a wallop?

INGREDIENTS

12 eggs
1 1/2 cups sugar
1 quart heavy cream
1 quart milk
1 quart bourbon, scotch, or apricot brandy
1 cup rum

DIRECTIONS

1. Separate the eggs.

2. Beat the egg whites together until stiff, then beat in a 1/2 cup of sugar.

3. Beat the egg yolks until pale and light.

4. Add the remaining cup of sugar and a 1/4 teaspoon of salt.

5. Combine the egg whites and egg yolks with the milk and bourbon.

6. Beat well, then add the rum.

7. Pour into a pitcher or jar and store in a cool place.

8. Shake or stir thoroughly before serving.

9. Sprinkle with nutmeg, if desired.

— Giving Love, adapted from a recipe in The Winter Solstice *by John Matthews*

Recipes: Sunday Brunch

Vegetable Frittata

INGREDIENTS

2 eggs per person plus a few extra (usually 3–4 dozen)
Vegetables on hand: onions, zucchini, carrots, spinach, broccoli, cabbage, etc.
Butter
Salt
Cheese

DIRECTIONS

1. Thinly slice the veggies.

2. Sauté in melted butter over medium heat until veggies are cooked but still firm.

3. Add salt to taste.

4. Meanwhile, crack all the eggs into a large bowl, add a bit of water or milk and beat until frothy.

5. *For scrambled-eggs style:*
   Pour eggs over veggies, stir and cook until done.
   Optional: when eggs are nearly done, add shredded cheese, cover and cook on low heat until cheese is melted.

6. *For baked-style:*
   Transfer partially cooked veggies into baking dish.
   Pour on the eggs, add salt to taste.
   Top with shredded cheese and bake at 350° for 15–20 minutes.

— *Craig Olson*

Wheel of the Year Scones

Ingredients

4 cups flour • 1/2 cup sugar
2 tablespoons baking powder
1 tablespoon ground cardamom
1 cup butter (2 sticks)
1 cup fresh or dried fruit
1/2 cup chopped nuts
1 cup milk • 2 eggs
1 teaspoon grated citrus peel — lemon,
    lime, or orange

Directions

1. Preheat oven to 400° F.
2. Mix together flour, sugar, baking powder and cardamom.
3. Cut 1 1/2-inch cubes of chilled butter into the flour mixture until well mixed.
4. Add one cup of fresh or dried fruit — diced apples, raisins, currants, dried or sweetened cranberries, frozen berries, and diced dates all work well.
5. Add 1/2 cup chopped nuts (optional).
6. Mix 2 eggs into 1 cup of milk, and add the juice of one lemon, lime, or half an orange (whatever you used for the fresh grated peel).
7. Pour over the flour mixture, fruit, and nuts. Mix until just moistened.
8. Separate into 4 portions. Pat each out into a circle about 1 inch thick.
9. Cut each of the 4 circles into 8 triangles — one for each of the 8 "tides" of the year. Will yield 32 scones.
10. Put on an ungreased cookie sheet. Brush each scone with a little milk/water and sprinkle with sugar and cinnamon.
11. Bake for 13 minutes or until golden brown. If you use fruits with lots of juice, such as fresh berries, the scones will take longer to bake.
12. Serve hot with butter or jam.

Note:

For our vegetarian or lactose intolerant friends this recipe works well with all kinds of milk (such as soy, almond, etc.), egg substitutes and dairy free butter. (Oils do not work well as fat substitutes.) I have made these successfully with *Bob's Red Mill Gluten-free Biscuit and Baking Mix* instead of flour, and omitted the baking powder. One package is about 4 cups — you can adjust the liquids down a little if the package is a little short in volume. I have also used honey and agave as well as various types of sugar successfully. Just wait to add liquid sweeteners at the time you add the rest of the liquids.

— *Debra Strom*

APPENDIX:

Why We Honor St Lucia

One of the most charming customs of the Yuletide season is that of the Lucy Bride. She is the young woman or girl who wears a crown of candles on her head and walks through the dimly lit home, carrying a tray of pastries and coffee to feed her family. She is called St. Lucia and is most commonly known as the Christian saint who was said to light the way to salvation. But why did this Italian saint, with her origins in Sicily, capture the hearts of the people of the far north? For it is in the dark, northern lands of Scandinavia that she is the most beloved. As Clement A. Miles wrote a hundred years ago, the imagery of the light shining forth out of darkness is a primary Yuletide theme, one that seems to strike deeply in the hearts of humankind. *"Lux in tenebris* is one of the strongest notes of Christmas: in the bleak midwinter a light shines through the darkness; when all is cold and gloom, the sky bursts into splendor, and in the dark cave is born the Light of the World."[1]

The historical Lucia was said to have been an early Christian martyr in Syracuse, Sicily, during the 4th century reign of Diocletian. She quickly became quite popular, with a widespread following by the 6th century. Two churches in Britain were dedicated to her before the 8th century, when Britain was still largely Pagan.

As with most saints, solid information about Lucia is lacking, but many stories and legends are told about her. It is said that Lucia came from a wealthy family, and that she carried food to persecuted Christians hiding in dark underground tunnels. She wore a wreath of candles on her head to light the way as she carried her baskets of provisions. Another legend says that she plucked out her own eyes and sent them to a suitor, so that she would not have to marry him. Yet another tale claims that she was tortured for her faith and was blinded in that manner, though God restored her eyesight in the end. Many images of St. Lucia show her holding a plate with eyeballs on it. She became the patron saint of the blind and those with eye trouble.

The emphasis on eyes may have come from the identification of the Sicilian woman Lucia with the Italic goddess of light, Lucina or Lucetia. This goddess was often pictured holding a lamp and a plate of cakes, which were later mistaken for eyeballs. Lucetia became known as one of the aspects of the Roman Queen of Heaven, Juno. As Juno Lucina, goddess of childbirth, she was known as the opener of the eyes of newborn children.

She was also known to feed her people in times of famine. A story is told that St. Lucia arrived in the Syracuse harbor in 1582, bearing wheat on a ship for the starving townsfolk who had prayed to her for help. A similar story takes place in medieval Sweden. St. Lucia, "with a face so radiant that there was a glow of light all about her head,"[2] arrived in a ship on Lake Vannern bearing provisions during a winter famine. From both of these stories comes the custom of eating wheat porridge in honor of Lucia.

> *How did the Italian Catholic saint travel to Lutheran Scandinavia and became firmly entrenched in Nordic culture? . . . It seems clear that the name Lucia, from* lux *(light), captured Northern hearts as she merged with their ancestral traditions of Freya and Frigga.*

Various explanations are given of how the Italian Catholic saint traveled to Lutheran Scandinavia and became firmly entrenched in Nordic culture. Did the Vikings bring the story of St. Lucia back with them on their travels? Perhaps the story was carried by German traders, or priests and monks from the British Isles may have introduced the story.

However the story arrived in the northlands, it seems clear that the name Lucia, from *lux* (light), captured Nordic hearts as she merged with their ancestral traditions of Freya and Frigga.

It was not unusual for the titles of ancient goddesses to be adopted as titles for both the Virgin Mary and for female saints. *Freya Vanadis,* meaning "shining bride of the gods," reminds us of Lucia's title "Lucy Bride." (There may also be a link to the Irish St. Brigit, or the Goddess Brigid, also known as Bride.) Frigga was known as "Queen of the Aesir," and St. Lucia was also called the "Lucia Queen." Both were solar goddesses, associated with sun symbols such as sunwheels, cats, spinning, amber, and gold. Freya was called *der vana solen,* "the beautiful sun," in a Swedish folksong.

The "eye" imagery of both Juno Lucina and the martyr Lucia is linked to Freya's eyes, which shed tears of amber in the ocean and gold on the earth. Unlike the virgin Lucia, however, who plucked out her eyes rather than submit to the caresses of a husband, Freya wept for her lost lover Odur. She was the giver of riches. One of Freya's names was "Gefjon," meaning "Giver" or "Allgiver," and she was known as the dispenser of wealth and plenty. It was said that her brother Frey gave the gift of fruitful fields while Freya gave the gift of crafted gold.

The golden saffron buns that the Lucy Bride serves are called *lussekatter,* literally "light cats." One Christian tale said that the "rolls served by Lucia were devil's cats which she subdued."[3] Freya's solar chariot was pulled by her famous cats across the heavens. These cats were known to control the sunshine — it was said that if it rained at an inconvenient time, it was because the neighborhood cats were peevish or hungry.

Frigga was more closely tied to hearth and home than Freya. She is the goddess of spinning and her symbols are the spindle and distaff. The act of spinning was considered a magical act, sometimes symbolizing the spinning of destinies by the Fates, sometimes the spinning of light by the sun goddess. The winter constellation we know as Orion was called "Frigga's Distaff," *Friggjar Rockr.* "As the spinner, [Frigga] appears in Austria under the thinly Christianized guise of 'St. Lucy' or *Spillelutsche,* 'Spindle-Lucia,' who, like Perchte, punishes those who have not spun during the year or have spun on her chosen feast-days."[4] Lucy, like Frigga, is the bringer of light and life to the household in the depths of winter.

"Lucia Morning" by Carl Larsson, 1908

> *"The Lucia Queen's visits drive away misfortune and bring good luck and prosperity."*

Freya and Frigga are both identified at times with the Germanic goddesses Holda and Berchta, who are the light and dark sides of the same being. Both Holda and Berchta forbade spinning or other rotary tasks during the Yuletide season, the time when the "sun stands still" (the meaning of the word "solstice"). In Christian times, the ban on spinning was extended to include St. Lucia's feast day.

Her feast day is December 13th, which was the day of the solstice before the change to the Gregorian calendar in the 1300s. An old English rhyme reminds us that St. Lucia's Day used to be the shortest day of the year: *"Lucy-light, Lucy-light, shortest day and longest night."* Today, her feast day is seen as the beginning of the holiday season and is often called Little Yule.

The choosing of a girl to embody the character of the *Lussibruden* (Lucy Bride) or "Lucia Queen" in her community dates back to the 12th century. She wears a white dress and red sash (symbolic of light and fire) and a wreath of greenery (lingonberry or whortleberry twigs) on her head. Candles are attached (some say nine, or seven, or four — all sacred numbers) to the wreath and lit. She sets out while it is still dark "to carry food and drink to every house in the parish, and also to visit stables and cow-byres, so that animals as well as human beings may share in the promise of lengthening days and greater plenty that she brings."[5] She is preceded by torchbearers, and followed by a train of maidens, "star boys," and wicked-looking trolls and demons. The goblins represent the bitter winter, soon to be vanquished by the radiant Lucia. "The Lucia Queen's visits drive away misfortune and bring good luck and prosperity."[6]

Besides the visits of the village Lucy Bride to all the homes in the community, each household has its own bright visitor. The oldest (or youngest) daughter arises "at first cockcrow," dons the gown, sash, and crown, and in the darkness before the dawn, awakens the sleeping family with songs, coffee, and special buns called *lussekatter*. Some families then eat breakfast in a kitchen lit with candles.

Since 1927, when a Stockholm newspaper sponsored a contest to choose the city's Lucy Bride, St. Lucia's Day has become a source of national pride in Sweden. Lucia processions are held in schools, hospitals, offices, and factories. There are Lucia contests where young women compete to represent their community. The winner of the Nobel Prize in Literature crowns Stockholm's St. Lucia.

An American woman of Swedish descent recalls the Lucia festivities of her own childhood: "I once knew a Swedish Evangelical Lutheran pastor . . . His predecessors, the Catholic priests, had taken five hundred years to clothe the [Lucia] tradition in its Christian trappings. St. Lucy was actually, he said, the goddess Freya. . . The pastor was quite old and had grown a bit testy as he spoke, and he finally rumbled that the Papists would never have been able to carry it off had they not struck on the device of placing at the center of their restructuring of the symbolism of this tradition a cup of hot, rich coffee and a slice of good coffee-cake."[7]

Whether or not her popularity is due to coffee and rolls, St. Lucia is greatly beloved as the Lightbringer during dark northern winters. Helen Farias neatly ties up all the elements of the Lucia story by saying that she "is the light-bringing midwife who is also bride, at the height of her power and who is most generous with her gifts, settling to earth at dawn in her cat-drawn chariot . . . just in time for breakfast."[8]

FOOTNOTES

1. Clement A. Miles, *Christmas Customs and Traditions,* Mineola, NY: Dover Publications, 1976/1912, p. 156.

2. Florence Ekstrand, *Lucia, Child of Light,* Mt. Vernon, WA: Welcome Press, 1989, p. 24.

3. Susan Granquist, "Lucy Fest," *Irminsul Aettir,* www.irminsul.org/arc/001sg.html (accessed 9/10/2010).

4. Alice Karlsdóttir, Stephan Grundy, Kveldulf Gundarsson, Melodi Lammond, Larsanthony K. Agnarsson, Karter Neal, Laurel Olson, Diana Paxson, Siegróa Lyfjasgy, and Dianne Luark Ross, "Chapter XIII: Frija and Other Goddesses," *Our Troth,* http://ourtroth.weebly.com/chapter-xiii-frija-and-other-goddesses.html (accessed 9/10/2010).

5. Christina Hole, *A Dictionary of British Folk Customs,* London: Paladin, 1976, p. 106.

6. Ibid.

7. Lynn H. Nelson, "Holiday Business All Done."

8. Helen Farias, "Festal Food: Lucia Cats," *TBP's Octava,* Vol. 1, No. 8, 1986.

BIBLIOGRAPHY

Freya Aswynn, *Northern Mysteries & Magick,* St. Paul, MN: Llewellyn Publications, 1998.

Helen Farias, "Customs and Legends of Little Yule," *TBP's Octava,* Vol. 5, No. 8, 1990.

Helen Farias, "Divine Mothers of a Northern Winter," *TBP's Octava,* Vol. 3, No. 7–8, 1988.

Helen Farias, "The Return of Lucia," *TBP's Octava,* Vol. 3, No. 1, 1987.

Helen Farias, "Magical Ladies of the Thirteen Nights," *The Beltane Papers,* Samhain 1992.

Waverly Fitzgerald, "St. Lucy's Day," *School of the Seasons,* www.schooloftheseasons.com/lucy.html (accessed 9/10/2010).

Waverly Fitzgerald and Helen Farias, *Midwinter,* Seattle: Priestess of Swords Press, 1995.

Stephan Grundy, Alice Karlsdottir, and Diana Paxson, "Chapter XVIII: The Frowe (Freyja)," *Our Troth,* http://ourtroth.weebly.com/chapter-xviii-the-frowe-freyja.html (accessed 9/10/2010).

Ellen Evert Hopman, *Tree Medicine Tree Magic,* Blaine, WA: Phoenix Publishing, 1992.

John Matthews, *The Winter Solstice: The Sacred Traditions of Christmas,* Wheaton, IL: Quest Books, 1998.

Patricia Monaghan, *O Mother Sun,* Freedom, CA: Crossing Press, 1994.

Thorskegga Thorn, "Spinning in Myths and Folktales," www.thorshof.org/spinmyth.htm (accessed 9/10/2010).

About Joanna Powell Colbert

Joanna Powell Colbert is an artist, author, retreat host, and teacher of tarot and earth-centered spirituality. *SageWoman* magazine recently named her as one of the Wisdom Keepers of the Goddess Spirituality Movement.

The Gaian Tarot, nine years in the making, combines Joanna's love of symbolic, archetypal art with the mysteries of the natural world. The Collector's Edition deck was released in 2010, and its run of 1000 is nearly sold out. A mass market version of the Gaian Tarot was published by Llewellyn Worldwide in 2011.

Joanna teaches e-courses and workshops on earth-centered spirituality, manifesting your dreams, the Sacred Feminine, seasonal contemplative practices, creativity as a devotional path, and using tarot as a tool for inner guidance and self-exploration. She also leads Gaian Soul Retreats for women twice a year, in the spring and fall.

Keep in touch:

www.gaiansoul.com • www.gaiantarot.com

Facebook: www.facebook.com/joannapowellcolbert

Twitter: www.twitter.com/joannapcolbert

Blessed Be!